RUN
WITH
THE
VISION

LESTER SUMRALL
with
J. Stephen Conn

4th printing 1990

RUN WITH THE VISION

Affectionately dedicated to my wife,
LOUISE LAYMAN SUMRALL
Who has untiringly, unselfishly and lovingly labored
with me in the gospel in many countries
and under many circumstances.

RUN
WITH THE
VISION

England, France, Jerusalem, Australia, Manila, Hong Kong, South Bend,
Indiana. With strong commitment and tirelessness of purpose, Lester
Sumrall has taken to heart the Lord's command to "go. . .into all the
world and preach the gospel to every creature."

At the age of seventeen, Lester faced two alternatives: death or the
ministry. It was then that he chose to preach—and the subsequent life
he's had has been remarkable beyond anyone's imagination.

Run With The Vision is the life story of a worldwide preacher whose
pulpit spans the globe and whose God loves all men whatever their
citizenship may be.

Lester Sumrall is fond of saying, "When you feed your faith, you starve
your doubts." This volume will be food for your faith.

PREFACE

A new book is something like a new gun. Until it is tested one is not sure of its precision or its strength. This story of a life lived for God is sent forth with eagerness that it shall reach the mark to bless, to heal, and to create faith.

During his days of hardship, Job did not realize he was living a book. His story became a book later. In the exciting adventures of my life the thought of placing them in print was not considered. My only thoughts were of victoriously accomplishing the tasks that God had given me to do.

From the time I was seventeen, I have sincerely sought to live in the will of God as revealed to me. I cannot remember a time when the Lord ever led me in any direction that I did not follow. This is one great reason for the variety of circumstances contained in this volume.

A constant inspiration of my life has been the three great keys to the life of the Apostle Paul. They are found in Romans 1:14-16.

In verse sixteen Paul said he was ''not ashamed of the gospel of Christ.'' In the church of his day were many shameful things. There was Ananias and Sapphira who were struck dead for lying. Then there was the group in Corinth who only came to church when their favorite minister came to town. But Paul was never ashamed of the gospel.

Whatever problems denominations have or whatever problems doctrines create, we go beyond them to say we are not ashamed of the pure and simple gospel of Christ. It is still the power of God unto salvation to all who believe.

The second key to Paul's life is in verse fifteen, "I am ready to preach the gospel in Rome." Paul was a true vigilante—a true minute man. When God spoke in the evening, he was on the trail by morning. He could declare with a clear conscience, "I was not disobedient unto the heavenly vision." Whether across seas or mountains or plains or bandit infested territory, Paul was ready. This I have sought to be—ever ready and willing for anything God desired of me.

The third key to Paul's life is the statement, "I am a debtor," verse fourteen. The apostle was not a debtor materially. He recognized a moral and spiritual debt to a paganistic, demonistic world that needed divine deliverance. He paid his debt by the day and never ceased paying that debt.

I have sought to walk in these three dimensions and I have learned that Christ is ever the same. All that He has done, He does today.

I trust that these chapters will create in you two desires: (1) To be holy before the Lord and pure in His sight; (2) to follow Him implicitly, without hesitation, so that when He speaks, we obey.

As I often say at the close of our daily telecast, "When you feed your faith, you starve your doubts." May this volume be food for your faith.

RUN
WITH
THE
VISION

1

The white headed physician breathed heavily, and slowly shook his head as he stood up after examining my seventeen-year-old, ninety-two pound frame. He motioned Papa over to the corner of my room and I listened in horror to his cold, guttural tone. "I'm going back to the office now," he said. "There's nothing more I can do. I can't even get a blood pressure reading or draw enough blood from his veins for a test."

For six months now the tuberculosis that ravaged my body had grown progressively worse. For the past several weeks I had been confined to bed. The doctor's visits had been frequent but futile. On that early autumn afternoon I had started to choke and turn blue in the face. Mother called Papa from his job at the machine shop to our home overlooking Saint Andrews Bay in Panama City, Florida.

I had been spitting blood every day for weeks. Even in the night, blood would run from my mouth and onto the pillow and bedclothes. Terrible night sweats mingled the stain of perspiration with the blood. But that afternoon it was much worse. Half-panfuls began to hemorrhage from one terrible heaving.

Mother and other loved ones stood now at the foot of my bed and wept. But their weeping did not prevent me from hearing the doctor again. "The boy is as good as dead now," I heard him say. "Call anyone you wish to see him. In two hours there will be no life left."

Two hours to live—it's the most frightening thing that could happen to a boy. My time had run out before it started; my life was over before it began. I had not had time to live and now it was time to die.

I wasn't ready to die—I knew that. I wasn't even ready to live. But I had run God's last red light and there was no place further to go.

The doctor picked up his bag to leave and turned again to my father. "I'll fill out the death certificate for Lester tonight and you can come by the office to pick it up in the morning. Then you can go down to the cemetery and choose a burial lot."

In my frightened, bewildered young mind I was aware of the door closing behind the doctor as he went out into the night.

This wasn't the first time I had been close to death. But it had never seemed so certain—so final. I can't say that my life necessarily flashed before me at that moment, but I was aware that on several previous occasions my life had been miraculously spared.

Just two or three years after I was born in New Orleans, Louisiana, in 1913, I was taken by the dreaded disease, pellagra. The doctor had told my mother I would die from this disease which was, at that time, extremely common among the "poor whites" of the South. This was years before doctors knew that pellagra was caused by a dietary deficiency and could be prevented by the inclusion of fresh fruits, vegetables, and milk in the daily meals.

Mother called the ladies from her prayer group at the church where she attended. They came to the house to pray for me and God answered them with a miracle. Later the doctor who had given me up to die saw me without any blotches, and could not believe it was the same child. God's cure left no defects from the ravaging disease.

At the age of five or six, I was playing on a railroad switching track near where we lived at the time in Laurel, Mississippi. I was totally unaware of the loose boxcar rolling down the track behind me in my direction. Suddenly, my oldest brother, Houston, more than twice my size, hit me and together we rolled off the track, inches ahead of the sharp steel wheels of the engineless freight car. Until that moment I had thought I was alone, oblivious to the danger that shadowed me.

A few years later I narrowly escaped death by drowning. It happened on a mild winter day when two friends and I decided to play hooky from school and walk down to the swimming hole near Laurel.

Winter rains had swollen the normally lazy waters of Tallahala Creek. The other boys, undeterred, challenged one another, "Let's swim across." The cool weather did not prevent them from stripping off "jaybird" and diving into the muddy current. I was the youngest and the last to dive in. My two stronger companions got across to the sandbank. I swam about halfway across but found my strength no match for the swollen stream. The current swiftly began to carry me away and as I weakened it sucked me completely under.

What happened in the next few moments I can only report from what was told me. One of the boys on the sandbank, the local preacher's son, panicked. "Let's get home; we're in trouble! He's gone!"

Lavert Hollifield, the other boy, protested. "No, I won't do that. Let's look for him."

"I'm not going to look for him," the preacher's kid answered, looking wide-eyed at the turbid foam that covered me. He left us.

Lavert dove in and felt along the sandy creek bottom until he found me, and with a desperate struggle dragged my body out onto the bank. I was not breathing and my lungs were filled with water. Lavert didn't know too much about artificial respiration. He just turned me over and punched my back until the mud and water gushed out and I gasped for air. He stayed there with me until my senses returned. Then together we made it back across the river to our clothes and Lavert helped me home.

Shortly after that, my family moved to Mobile, Alabama, and once again, I flirted with death. It was February, Mardi Gras time in Mobile, and I was sixteen. That night I wore a mask and a new heavy, navy blue sweater, running through the streets of the city with two other boys. The whole town seemed to be going crazy. We were running and screaming and looking for mischief, when it found us. A little creature that looked like a girl, although you couldn't be sure, came up and hit me. I spun around and walloped her with my fist, knocking her flat onto the street. The next thing I knew the guy who was with her pulled a long razor and slashed out at me. I fell backwards and as I did the razor sliced clean through my thick sweater and shirt, cutting it all the way down the front. The girl got up and they both ran away, not knowing whether they had cut me or not. But once again I had escaped the death angel's call.

I was aware of these times that I had a scrape with death, and now as the doctor was leaving our house to fill out my

14

death papers, I thought my luck had finally run out—that the end had come.

At that moment God gave me a vision. It was the most dramatic and significant thing that would ever happen to me. I looked to the right side of my bed and there, suspended in midair, was a casket. I was not dreaming, nor was I asleep. It was bright, vivid, real. It was even beautiful, lined with soft silk and bedecked with white lilies and red roses all around. The casket was turned up just a little so that I could see inside. It was empty, and I was impressed that it was just my size.

I had never seen a vision before. It frightened me. Fitfully I turned onto my left side, hoping to escape.

There on the left, resting in midair beside my bed, was an open Bible. It was as big as my bed, larger than any book I had ever seen. And without being told I knew that the Bible meant that I was to preach.

God spoke to me at that moment, as I glanced feverishly back to the casket and then again to the open book. "Lester, which of these will you choose tonight?"

It was not an audible voice. Yet it was as distinct and firm as any voice I had ever heard. God was giving me a choice.

I wanted to be anything but a preacher. I despised preachers. I wasn't even a Christian. At the same time, I was horrified at the thought of dying. To me the open casket meant much more than just a grave. It meant hell—everlasting torment. I had heard enough preaching to know if I died that night, hell would be my eternal destiny.

Not being ready to die, I wanted to live at any cost. Looking straight at the Bible I prayed, "God, if the only way in the world for me to live is to preach—I'll preach." And then to confirm what I had just said, I added, "If you will let me live as long as I preach, one day I will be the oldest man in the world, because I won't ever stop preaching.''

I meant it. That commitment to preach was also my commitment to give my heart to Jesus Christ. I accepted both His calling and His full salvation. It was settled.

The vision was over. As I drifted into a deep, sweet slumber there was a sense of destiny. My life had been preempted by a higher power.

I was the only one in our house who slept much that night. As I rested in peace the finger of God touched my lungs and healed them. When I opened my eyes to the next morning's light, my dear mother stood over my bed. She had kept her vigil throughout the night. Her eyes were blurry from weariness and weeping, and I had never seen her look more beautiful. My fever was gone. And there was not one drop of blood on my pillow.

Mother, seeing that I was awake, asked if there was anything she could do.

''I'm hungry,'' I smiled at her. It was the first time I had been hungry in weeks.

Mother turned toward the kitchen, ''I'll get you some grape juice.''

''Oh, no, Mother,'' I called back to her. ''I've had all the grape juice I want for a long, long time.''

''What do you want, Lester?''

''What did Papa have for breakfast?''

She told me that he had eaten ham and eggs, hot biscuits, grits, and red-eye gravy.

Hearing her describe Papa's breakfast made me more hungry than ever. ''That's what I want.''

Mother began to cry again. ''Oh no, no, no. You haven't had any heavy food in your stomach and you would die!''

I grinned weakly at her and teased, "Well, I want to die full of ham and eggs and hot buscuits, and gravy—with grits."

Mother replied hesitantly, "Well, the doctor said you are going to die anyway. I'll give you what you asked. At least your last desire will be granted."

She prepared the huge hot breakfast that I had ordered. And when she sat it down beside my bed she turned her back and began to sob again.

I ate. Oh, how I ate! I cleaned my plate and asked for a second helping. Mother insisted, "Let's wait and see if this hurts you." But it didn't hurt me.

I explained, "Mother, I have seen a vision." I told her about the casket and the great open book, and I looked her in the face and said, "Mother, I am going to be a preacher."

That little shouting mother of mine was overjoyed. All her prayers for seventeen years suddenly came true. She began to rejoice in the Lord. She had a right to rejoice.

"Oh, Lord, I thank you; I thank you. I knew you would do it!" She lifted her hands in thanksgiving and praise as her heart bubbled over. Mother was elated that I had been healed of tuberculosis. But she was even more exuberant that her rebellious prodigal had come "home."

Mother had prayed for me since I could remember. During family devotions I had often heard her pray, "Lord, please make Lester a preacher."

Afterwards I would beg her, "Mother, don't pray that."

Two of my older brothers, Houston and Ernest, were already ministers and were pastoring churches.

Mother had been brought up in a Methodist home, and as a young girl she felt the call of God on her life to become a missionary to China. She still regretted that she had followed the advice of her pastor who told her, "A woman has no place on the mission field." He suggested that she become a business secretary—which she did.

Later Mother had received the baptism of the Holy Spirit. Although Papa did not receive Christ at that time, she was faithful to take her seven children to a Full Gospel church and Sunday school.

Anna, my oldest sister, had also felt an urgent call of the Lord to be a missionary to China. But Anna refused God's call and married a sinner. She died at an early age.

I was next to the baby of the family, Leona being the youngest. The two of us were the only ones left at home now. Of all her children, I had been my mother's greatest heartache. I was disobedient, rebellious, and had a hot, fast temper. In her frustration, Mother had even threatened to send me to a detention home. But most of all, she loved me and prayed for me.

Several had been the occasions when I would return home at two o'clock in the morning, after a night of reveling with my friends, to stumble over my mother's feet as I groped for my bed in the darkness.

"What are you doing in my room?" I would ask.

"I'm praying for you, Lester," Mother would answer, and go down to the living room to continue her prayer. I didn't sleep easy on those nights. In my heart I knew even then that God had a higher plan for my life than I had for myself.

My strength returned quickly after my healing. I had fresh air and sunshine in abundance from the twenty-four windows that formed the walls of my room overlooking Saint Andrews Bay and the Gulf of Mexico. The fresh air and sunshine had not been sufficient for my healing. That had taken the touch of God.

In three days I was walking all over the house and eating everything my mother would prepare for me. In ten days I was out in a boat on the gulf, fishing with a friend. Life was quickly returning to normal.

It was on a morning only three weeks following my vision and healing that I was praying in my room and God spoke to me a second time. "You promised me you would preach if I healed you," His voice impressed me. "What are you waiting for?"

With a sudden sense of urgency I rushed downstairs to where my father was eating breakfast and announced, "Papa, I'm going to go out and preach. I'm going today."

Papa was really upset. He snorted and raved and threatened. "You're not going to do any such thing. You're not strong enough to go. You wouldn't know anything to say if you did go."

My father wasn't a Christian man. His low opinion of preachers in general was reflected when he fumed, "I don't want all my sons to be beggars. Preachers are out begging for a living." He hit the table and cursed, "I want you to have a real job. Why do you think I have already spent a lot of good money to teach you a trade?"

"No, Papa. I've got to go and preach."

"You're not going to do it."

"But God said I had to preach."

"God nothing!" That 225-pound Irish father of mine jumped from his chair in a rage. My spirit withered like a leaf and I just stood there trembling and weeping. I was shattered.

Finally I turned and ran back up the stairs to my room. The last words I heard him yell after me were, "You would starve to death if you went!"

In the sanctuary of my bedroom I fell on the floor and cried. "My heavenly Father says 'go,' and my earthly father says 'no.' What can I do Lord?"

Through my tears God impressed upon my mind Isaiah 41:10 and 11. I had never read those verses before and I had no idea what they were about. But that still, small voice was so definite that I spread my Bible open before me on the floor and began to read.

"Fear thou not; for I am with thee. . ."

As I read that promise something instantly changed inside me. God's love overwhelmed me. He reached down and took fear out of my being. Now I was laughing and crying at the same time. It took me about an hour to regain my composure enough to finish reading the verses:

". . .be not dismayed; for I am thy God: I will strengthen thee; yea, I will help thee; yea, I will uphold thee with the right hand of my righteousness.

"Behold, all they that were incensed against thee shall be ashamed and confounded: they shall be as nothing; and they that strive with thee shall perish."

"All right, God," I said aloud, "if you're going with me, I'm ready to go."

I went to the closet and pulled out a little forty-nine cent brown, fiberboard suitcase. It didn't take long to fill it with what few clothes I had. My father had already left for work when I marched downstairs again, suitcase in hand.

"Where are you going?" my mother wanted to know.

"Out to preach."

"But, son, where are you going to preach? You have nowhere to go."

"I don't know where I'm going, Mother, but I've got to go." I kissed her goodbye and walked out onto the front porch. I would never return to that house again.

A young friend of mine who owned an old jalopy car was in front of the house. Today I can't even remember his name. I told him where I was going and he volunteered to go with me. Why not? He had nothing else to do. Together we chugged up the road. I was not at all sure of our destination but I was compelled by an unexplainable pressure of destiny. I had to be obedient to that heavenly vision. And I knew that I was not alone.

2

My friend and I headed north in his old Overland car. I was too naive to know that a newly converted, seventeen-year-old boy couldn't just go out and preach without any preparation, and without a church to preach in.

We nursed the old jalopy up the road having to stop every five miles to refill the radiator with water. We were growing hungry when at one stop we spotted a persimmon tree standing beside the road, hanging heavy with its bright orange fruit. We shook the tree of its ripe bounty, then sat down in the grass underneath and ate our fill. Our faith and our spirits were high at that moment. We imagined how Elijah must have felt after being fed by the ravens by the brook Cherith.

We had not traveled more than forty or fifty miles from Panama City when we noticed a little, white, one-room frame schoolhouse sitting out in the middle of a cotton patch. Something inside me said, "That's the place." We stopped and inquired at a nearby farmhouse to learn who was in charge of the school building.

Upon finding the farmer who kept the key, I asked in my most polite but authoritative voice, "Sir, we want to use that schoolhouse to preach in."

I must not have looked too much like a preacher to the old farmer as I stood there in all my ninety-two pounds of city-boy finery. The farmer glanced first at my peach fuzz complexion, then at my clean, manicured fingernails, and down to my neatly pressed white trousers. I couldn't tell whether the expression on his face reflected bewilderment or amusement—maybe a little of both.

Perhaps I had better explain a bit more to him, I thought. "I've been sick of tuberculosis and if I don't preach I'll die of tuberculosis. God healed me to preach."

He was still looking at me sort of funny so I continued with a threat. "If you don't let me have that schoolhouse to preach in then I will die and you will be to blame."

At that the poor farmer's mouth dropped open and the tobacco juice ran out the side and dribbled down onto his chin. "Now son," he drawled, with a twinkle in his eye, "I wouldn't want you to die."

"Well, let us have the schoolhouse." I failed to see the humor in it.

He rummaged around in his pockets and came out with an old key that fit the schoolhouse door. We thanked him, then under our breath we thanked the Lord, and started to go.

As an afterthought I turned and asked, "Would you mind loaning us a lantern too?" He let us have the lantern. That night revival began in the old country schoolhouse, I as the evangelist and my friend as the song leader.

After getting the key, we just went up and down the road telling everyone we saw about the meeting. Eight farmers were present the first night. Word of the revival spread rapidly throughout the countryside and the crowds grew night after night.

On the first evening of the revival one of the farmers

invited us to stay in his home. After a day or two he greeted me gruffly one morning at the breakfast table. ''Boy, in my house if you don't work, you don't eat.''

I thought I had been working, preaching every night, and preparing for the services during the daytime. The farmer saw it differently. He handed me two big pails with ''Standard Oil'' printed on them and ordered, ''Here, take these slop buckets and go feed my pigs.''

I wasn't accustomed to that type of work but I soon learned. It was a few hundred yards from the house down to the pigpen. As I carried the heavy buckets, the foul smelling ''slop'' sloshed over onto my clothes and into my shoes and all over my pride. By the time I got down to where the pigs were kept I was upset and angry at the world.

I didn't even know how to call hogs. I just yelled, ''Come and get it.'' They came. And as the pigs grunted and made hogs of themselves tears ran down my cheeks. ''Oh, God, I thought I was a prodigal son and now I know it.''

Setting the empty buckets down in the mud beside the pigpen, I went out into the corn patch nearby. I begged, ''Please, God, let me go back home. Or let me die right here. Anything, Lord—but not this.''

It's not that I minded working. From the age of twelve I had always worked and made my own way. My parents were both able and willing to provide for me, but making money just happened to be one of the things I enjoyed doing most.

On my own initiative I used to go to the local wholesale house and buy 100-pound bags of peanuts. I would take these home, parch them in the oven, put them into small paper bags, and sell them to the men who worked in the lumber mill near our home.

In the summertime I would build myself a wagon from scrap parts and cover it with a canvas top. I then would pull the wagon down to the icehouse for a block of ice. Taking different flavors of heavy syrup, an ice scraper, and paper cups, I was set up in the snowball business.

I would pay a boy fifty cents a day to pull the wagon while I walked behind doing the scraping and selling. At five cents a snowball, I often cleared three or four dollars per day. Back then, when a dollar was a dollar, that was good money for a boy—or for anyone.

At the age of sixteen I dropped out of high school and entered Mobile Beauty and Barber College. I worked so hard at becoming a hairdresser that after only six or eight weeks they gave me the first chair. When we moved to Panama City, I was hired to operate the front chair in the main shop downtown, where I stayed until my tuberculosis became too bad. I loved to work, and I had a passion for making money.

But this preaching business was no way to make a living. The offerings were miserably small. I preached for literally pennies a night. One entire week I collected only thirty cents, twenty-five pennies and a nickel. Another week I got only twenty-six pennies and not a single nickel. Even at that, some folks complained that I was being overpaid. ''The gospel should be free,'' they said. Even in those depression days, I could make more in one day selling snowballs than in a whole month of preaching. And here I was having to slop hogs for my room and board.

To add insult to injury, I didn't even like being a preacher. From childhood I had learned to despise the ministry.

When I was a boy, evangelists didn't know anything about hotels. If a visiting minister came to a church he always stayed with ''the saints.'' And at our church that usually meant he stayed with the Sumralls. It always seemed to be our good fortune to live near the church.

Revivals in those days were genuine "protracted meetings," continuing sometimes three or four months. Most of the evangelists who stayed with us impressed me as rough, crude, poorly educated men. Worse than that, when they stayed at our house I lost my bed. I had to sleep on a pallet, just a couple of quilts spread on the wood floor. As a young boy I would often go to sleep lying on the hard church benches, while the services lasted until 10:30 or 11:00 P.M. Then I would be awakened and carried home only to be put on a hard pallet for the rest of the night. That was okay for a night or two, but after a period of weeks I grew to resent it. Most of all I resented the evangelist who slept in my bed.

Also, the evangelist robbed me of my place beside my father at the dinner table. During revivals I would have to eat at the "second table" after the grownups had finished their meal. And one thing about those old-time preachers— they really ate. I sometimes wondered if there would be enough left for me.

I retaliated by stealing from the evangelists' pockets, tinkering with their automobiles to keep them from starting, and shooting out the lights in their revival tents. One day I became totally fed up with one evangelist who had a particularly large family with him. I got hold of his boy, about my size, and poured sorghum molasses into his hair. I then dusted flour onto the gooey mess and rubbed it in, demanding, "Now tell your father I want him to please leave town."

Instead of leaving town the evangelist just called for special fasting and prayer for Lester to try to get him saved.

Up until a few weeks before that morning when I found myself crying and praying prostrate in the cornfield, I hated preachers. Now I was one. And I wasn't at all sure that I didn't hate myself, too.

However, as I prayed I felt an assurance that I was doing the work that God had ordained me to do. I heard His still, small voice within, "If you will be patient, I will do many wonderful things for you." I got up from the corn field with a renewed determination to preach, whatever the cost.

I really didn't know anything about how to prepare a sermon. The first several nights I just told about my vision and healing. As the people began to tire of hearing that same testimony, I started telling Bible stories I remembered from Sunday school, the story of David, the prodigal son, etc. I would read the Bible all day and then just get up and talk from it at night. I was growing spiritually day by day.

It wasn't long before I developed a method of illustrating my sermons by having people from the congregation dress and act out the parts of the Bible characters as I preached about them. That seemed to create interest and perk up the attendance.

Actually we never thought about not having a crowd. The people were always there. In those days there was little in the way of competition such as television, places of amusement, etc. A revival meeting often provided the only entertainment that many poor country folk could afford.

Bible prophecy was one of the most popular evangelistic themes in those depression days. Communism had recently been born in Russia and President Roosevelt had just inaugurated the N.R.A. (National Recovery Administration). People were hungry to hear about these and other current events in the light of Bible prophecy. I began to study the newspapers along with my Bible and declared the end-time message.

That first schoolhouse revival lasted for six weeks and at the close we took eighty-seven adults down to the creek and baptized them by immersion. I didn't know what to do with my converts so I just left them. They kept holding services and a church was established from the effort.

From that revival I went twenty or thirty miles on up the road to another—and then another. Invitations began to come for me to minister in churches as well as schoolhouses. From one rural community to another I worked my way up through Mississippi and into Tennessee and Arkansas.

The young man who started out with me married a lovely young lady and settled down. I have not seen him since. Within a year I was joined by my younger sister, Leona. She added much to the meetings by playing her guitar and singing.

God miraculously blessed our efforts and wherever we went the whole countryside was stirred. From one revival two missionaries went to Africa. Many other young men and women were called into the gospel ministry.

One thing that troubled me deeply during those first months as an evangelist was that I had not yet received the baptism in the Holy Ghost. I was well acquainted with the doctrine but not the blessing. One of the first sounds I ever remembered hearing was that of my godly mother speaking in an unknown tongue as the Spirit gave the utterance. Having been reared around Full Gospel people all my life I thought that receiving the Holy Ghost would be no problem. But it didn't come that easy for me.

Sometimes I would go ahead and preach about the Holy Spirit, not from my own experience, but from the Acts of the Apostles. I admonished others that they should seek for the blessing. Many of them did—and received. Of course this caused some controversy. People would say, "He has no right to preach about the Holy Ghost. He doesn't even have the Holy Ghost himself." Others would point to me and mock, "Here's a man who doesn't live what he preaches." They were right. I was open about my lack and that brought much criticism.

Desperately I sought the infilling of the blessed Holy Spirit during those months. Often after preaching I myself would be among the seekers at the altar. It was the craziest thing you've ever seen. I doubt if any pastor would have allowed that kind of circus in his church.

After others had received the Holy Ghost, then they would come over to where I was seeking and try to "pray the preacher through." They would lay their hands on me and instruct me to repeat hallelujah or glory, glory, glory!

In my heart I rebelled against this method. I didn't want the Holy Ghost to come as a result of working myself into a frenzy. I felt that it should be supernatural—from God.

The day I finally received the Holy Spirit I was preaching on the front porch of a country schoolhouse outside of Fayetteville, Arkansas. The sponsoring group had no pastor and I was staying with a German farmer.

I was particularly discouraged. After preaching that evening, ten people had been saved and seven received the Holy Spirit. I had been down at the altar seeking with the rest of them, but I didn't receive anything.

I went back to the room where I was staying and lay on the bed disgusted. As I stared up at the bedroom ceiling, I mumbled aloud to myself. "Here I talk about this and I don't have it. What's wrong with me?"

The Lord began to deal with me. "You have felt that you could just grab anything you wanted when and how you wanted it," I heard Him say. You see, I had fasted often for the infilling of the Holy Spirit. I somehow had the notion that a person could get anything he desired just by fasting for it. I had tried to earn the Holy Ghost.

God continued to speak to my heart. "Since you didn't receive the Holy Ghost your way, now I am going to give the Spirit to you as a free gift."

I wasn't even praying for the Holy Ghost at that moment. I was just lying there half mad and feeling sorry for myself. All of a sudden the glory of God came into that room as I had never felt it before. The Spirit seemed to flow from the corner of the room until it touched the foot of my bed, my feet, and came up through me. As it did, I began to speak in a heavenly language I never learned. My efforts to receive the Holy Ghost in my own strength had ended in frustration. Now with no effort of my own, God filled me by His grace. I went to sleep rejoicing in my newfound prayer language.

The next morning I announced to the folks where I was staying, "I received a blessing last night."

The lady of the house answered, "Everybody knows it!" Nothing more was said.

I remained faithful to my calling as a preacher—maybe more faithful than was necesssary. I did not take a vacation or even return home for a rest or a visit. My folks did come to visit me from time to time. I preached nonstop, closing one meeting on a Sunday night and starting somewhere else on Monday.

I had always been a strong competitor. In school I had boxed, wrestled, played football, basketball, baseball, every sport available. I played rough. I played to win. And I loved it. Even years later as a preacher I still enjoyed sports whenever the opportunity came to participate. I threw myself into my preaching with the same enthusiastic abandon.

My preaching style in those days as a teenage evangelist was enthusiastic, to say the least. When I preached, I would jump or run and yell loudly at the sinners to repent. My voice would grow hoarse and my body became drenched with sweat. The Deep South was a violent place to live in the early 1930s. I had a violent life before my conversion and now I preached according to the man that I was and the disposition God had given me.

In spite of my hard work and faithfulness, I had a bad attitude about the ministry. My motive was almost altogether negative. I was preaching just to stay alive—to keep from dying of tuberculosis. I was unhappy with my lot as a minister. As a result, sometimes I didn't try very hard to be nice to people. Oftentimes after wailing away at them from the pulpit I would say, "You have heard my sermons. Now your getting saved is not part of my deal with God. He just told me to preach. Whether or not you get saved is your business."

One night I asked a young woman, "Do you want to go to heaven?" She shook her head no. Almost in anger at her refusal, I told her bluntly, "Then you go to hell." I turned around and walked to the front of the building. I looked back and saw that she had fainted and fallen to the floor.

After some ladies brought her to, I went to her and said, "You seemed healthy enough when I was back here before. What happened to you!"

She answered , "I never had anybody tell me to go to hell before, let alone the preacher."

I said, "Lady, there are only two places to go and you told me you didn't want to go to one of them, so you're bound to go the the other." I did get a convert that night in spite of my brashness.

For the first eighteen months of my ministry my attitude was terrible. I had been like a Gramophone, grinding out a message each night with no compassion, with no feeling; but I guess the Lord knows He can keep working and polishing us—filling us with Himself—until He gets us fit for His service. I marvel now to look back and realize how God used that early ministry in spite of my abruptness and negativism.

After about eighteen months of preaching just to keep from dying, God miraculously changed the entire course of my ministry, and my life.

It happened in one dramatic evening. God gave me a second vision—the only other vision I have had during my spiritual life.

It was in a little frame church building in the Tennessee countryside. I was sitting to the side of the pulpit where a young man stood waving his arms and leading the congregation in song.

Suddenly I was no longer aware of the church, the people, or the song they were singing. I saw before me all the people of the entire world. They were wearing their native clothing and they were every shade of black and brown and red and white. I was impressed with how beautiful they were as they walked down a very long and wide highway leading away from me. It was very real. I could not believe I was experiencing a vision until after it was ended and I found myself back in the little building.

I had never seen a large missionary pageant before and

many of the native costumes were strange to me, yet in the Spirit I was able to tell the countries of the world they represented.

In the vision, God lifted me up until I was looking down upon that uncountable multitude of humankind. He took me far down the highway until I saw the end of the road. It ended abruptly at a precipice towering above a bottomless inferno. When the tremendous unending procession of people came to the end of the highway I could see them falling off into eternity. As they neared the pit and saw the fate that awaited them, I could see their desperate but vain struggle to push back against the unrelenting pressure of those to the rear. The great surging river of humanity swept them ever forward.

God opened my ears to hear the screams of damned souls sinking into hell. God brought me nearer. As men and women of all nations plunged into that awful chasm, I could see their faces distorted with terror. Their hands flailed wildly, clawing at the air.

As I beheld in stunned silence, God spoke to me out of the chaos. "You are responsible for these who are lost."

"No, not me, Lord," I defended myself. "I do not know these people. I have never been to Japan, or China, or India; I am not to blame."

God's voice was tender yet firm as he spoke again. "When I say unto the wicked, Thou shalt surely die; and thou givest him not warning, nor speakest to warn the wicked from his wicked way, to save his life; the same wicked man shall die in his iniquity; *but his blood will I require at thine hand.*"

That was the shortest sermon I had ever heard—and the most frightening. It was preached to me by God himself. Not until later did I discover that the passage was in the Bible (Ezekiel 3:18).

"Oh, God," I said. "Do you mean I can be responsible for Africans going to hell even though I have never been to Africa? Am I responsible for South Americans being lost when I have never been there?"

God left no doubt in my mind. I was impressed that every Christian is responsible for taking the message of God's grace and salvation to those who have never heard.

Suddenly the vision was over. I was still trembling. Opening my eyes, I saw that the meeting house was dark and I was there alone. I supposed the people had decided I was praying in a trance and just closed the meeting and left me. It didn't matter. A heavy burden settled down over my soul and my heart felt like it was breaking in two. I began to weep, heaving and sobbing uncontrollably from deep inside. I had cried before, but I didn't know a human could cry as I did that night. I prostrated myself on that wooden floor and remained there all night agonizing before the Lord.

"Oh, God," I implored, "forgive me, forgive me for not loving the least, the last, and the lost of this world."

I made a covenant with God that I would run as no man had ever run; I would fight as no man had ever fought, to find the lost and bring them the good news. From that night I knew that the world would be my parish.

When I walked out of that little building at eight o'clock the next morning I had to push my eyes open where I had cried them shut. I was a new man. Something had matured in my soul that night. I felt that I had been sanctified, set apart by God for a particular purpose.

Friends told me that I spoke differently, my words possessed a new authority, and at the same time they contained a tenderness that had not been there before. God had given me a compassion and an urgency for souls that would never fade as long as I preached.

Just over a year from that eventful night, at the age of twenty, I began active missionary work that would eventually lead me into over one hundred nations of the world and to every continent of the earth. The soles of my feet would slap the streets of over one thousand of the world's great cities, teaming with their frustrations, disease and sins. And everywhere I went I would declare the blessed hope of eternal life through Jesus Christ.

It would not be all glory. A long, lonely, rugged road lay before me. I could not even dream of the adventures of faith and miracles that God had in store for me. From this divine compassion there would be no turning back. For the rest of my days I must run with the vision.

3

At the same time that God was giving me the vision of a world going to hell, a man by the name of Howard Carter, living in London, England, was in prayer. The date was December 18, 1931. Howard Carter, in his early forties, was general superintendent of the Assemblies of God in Great Britain and Ireland, and the president of Hampstead Bible Institute. As he prayed that evening, God gave him a prophecy concerning a helper who would assist him in his work. The words of this message so impressed him that he wrote them down:

I have found one for thee, yea, I have called a worker to stand beside thee. He hath heard my call, he respondeth, he joineth thee in the work to which I have called thee. I have called him, although thou hast not seen him. He is called and chosen and shall join thee. Behold he cometh, he cometh from afar; he cometh to help thee to carry thy burden and be a strength at thy side, and thou shalt find pleasure in his service and shall delight in his fellowship. He shall come at the time appointed and shall not tarry; at a time thou thinkest not shall he appear, even when thou art engaged in my work.

The next morning at a staff meeting of the Bible Institute, Howard Carter told of the prophecy he had received, and then read it.

One of the professors responded, "You are going to get married. God is going to bring you a pretty woman from some far country."

Howard Carter said, "Oh? Let me read it again." So he read, "Behold *he* cometh, *he* cometh from afar, *he* cometh to help thee. . . ." The prophecy didn't say anything about a woman at all. God was going to send a man to travel with him.

1932 passed as did the next year. Each day Howard Carter expected the helper to arrive, but the promise remained unfulfilled. In 1934, he received an invitation to the United States to speak at the tri-state camp meeting in Eureka Springs, Arkansas. This invitation he refused because he felt it was a waste of time to travel so far. But before his letter of rejection was received (there was no transatlantic airmail in those days), a cablegram was sent asking if he was planning to accept the invitation. The wording of that cablegram convinced Mr. Carter that it was the will of the Lord for him to go. He cabled back, "Ignore letter, am accepting."

Mr. Carter's missionary secretary in London suggested that he should extend his trip to visit the missionaries in the Far East before returning home. Feeling that the missionaries needed to be visited, he decided to seek for divine guidance in the matter. He borrowed the key to a church near the Bible school, locked himself in the building, and spent several hours with God in prayer and fasting. God gave him the spiritual direction he sought in the form of another prophecy:

"Prepare thou for the journey and clothe thee for the path which thou shall take, for I am sending thee and I will go with thee. Thou hast waited for me, and thou hast done well, for thy waiting has been thy wisdom, and thou hast shown knowledge of my way. I will go with thee to prepare the path and will give thee grace to tread it. Thou shalt speak my words and shalt follow my leading and do my will.

"Place after place thou shalt visit and shalt comfort my people and gather mine elect together, for I am sending thee. Let not another say, "He sendeth thee," for I am sending thee, saith the Lord, and I am providing thee with all thou needest. To the nations, I am sending thee, to the countries where my servants labor. Thou shalt comfort my people and cheer those who have labored for me. In dark places shalt thou give them help, for I am with thee."

Assured by this message, Howard Carter sailed for New York in early June. First he preached at a camp meeting at Santa Rosa, California, and then worked his way back to Eureka Springs, Arkansas.

In the meantime I was continuing my work as a youth evangelist, with the call of world evangelism burning hot within me. I was restlessly waiting for God to open the door for me to fulfill the vision. I wanted to get to the nations so badly I didn't know what to do. I would preach to Americans and see Chinese. At other times as I preached, everyone in the place would appear black. I was preaching to Africans. I would stand before the people with tears running down my cheeks because I was crying for the heathen. But no missions board was willing to send an unproven teenage evangelist.

It was while I was preaching a revival in Oklahoma that I learned of Howard Carter's coming to preach the tri-state camp meeting. As I was praying one night, God impressed me to close out the revival and go to Eureka Springs. I didn't know anything about Howard Carter—or anything about the camp meeting for that matter, yet I was sure of God's directive. When I went to church that night I told the pastor that I was closing the meeting.

He became angry. "That's just the trouble with you new little preachers. You don't have any respect for your elders. You don't do what you're told. You promised to be here and you should be here."

I explained to him that I really wanted to finish the revival but I was compelled to go. He never did understand. The next morning Leona and I drove out of Oklahoma and found our way to the Eureka Springs campground.

Upon arriving we went into the large hall just in time to hear Howard Carter lecturing on the "Gifts of the Spirit." It was while in a prison for being a conscientious objector during World War I that God had revealed to him the phenomenal truth of the gifts of the Holy Spirit. Today the entire charismatic world follows his teachings on the gifts. Every book that has been written on the subject can be traced back to Howard Carter's influence. I had never heard anyone teach on the gifts before that morning and I was amazed at what I heard.

Outside on the sidewalk after the service I shook hands with Howard Carter and introduced myself. Then after what seemed to be a long moment of silence, I began to speak very strange things that I myself didn't understand. As I was speaking what seemed to me to be foolishness, I suddenly stopped and apologized. "I'm sorry, sir. I don't usually talk like this to people."

"I know it," he smiled at me. "Come with me to my room and I will tell you why you have spoken as you have."

Many years later in an article which appeared in *World Harvest Magazine,* Howard Carter told of the first encounter with me on the sidewalk: "His words excited me. He was repeating the message God had given me in London which I had read the night before while in prayer. . . .When I heard the very words of the Lord's message to me flowing from his lips, I was immediately convinced that a miracle was taking place. I grew excited, but let me hasten to explain that my excitement was of a very conservative nature, for I did not betray the slightest evidence of emotion. But the matter certainly amazed me and I said within myself that this young man was, without doubt, the one of whom the Lord had spoken in 1931."

When Mr. Carter led me to his room, he pulled out a book of prophecies from his suitcase, opened it and shared with me that the words I had spoken were the very words God had given to him in London many months earlier. Then he looked straight at me and said, "You're the one."

He then began to explain to me his procedure in the work of God regarding finance. Since entering the ministry, Howard Carter said that he had never on any occasion asked for any fee for preaching. He never mentioned his personal needs to anyone but only to the Lord. He made it clear that if I were to travel with him it would be by faith. Each of us would pay his own way as we traveled around the world. We would depend upon God to meet our needs through His people, but we would never ask for help or give hints of our need. I was happy to follow his arrangements respecting finance, for God had already been teaching me to live that way. We knew it was necessary for two to agree before they walked together.

Immediately I left for Mobile, Alabama, where my parents were now living, to leave my sister, Leona, and make arrangements for the trip. After selling my car and securing a passport, I caught a train to California. My family was upset to say the least. My father thought I was crazy to go out in the ministry as I had done, and now he knew I was crazy to start off around the world with the gospel.

When I arrived in Los Angeles, Howard Carter had already departed America. I was to hear of his whereabouts at the Bethel Temple church, where he had held a meeting. Dr. Turnbull, the Bethel Temple pastor, told me that he thought Mr. Carter had gone to Japan. Another pastor said that he had gone to China, and another felt sure that it was India. I had no idea where Howard Carter was but I felt certain that God wanted me to go with him, so I traveled up to San Francisco and bought a ticket on a steamer to China. (Later I would learn that Mr. Carter had written me of his last minute change of plans to go first to Australia. But I had not received the letter.)

That night when I went to my room I was very unsettled about going to China. I prayed, "I don't know where he is, Lord. What shall I do?" While praying I felt a strong impression from the Lord to buy a ticket to the bottom of the world and work my way up. But some of my luggage was already on the boat bound for Hong Kong. I had already been asked to speak at the religious services on Sunday while at sea and in only two more days we would be leaving port.

What could I do? I had spent almost all the money from the sale of my car to buy the ticket to China. The steamship company's policy was to give no refunds. Sitting in the city square of San Francisco, I prayed for God to help me. Then I went to the office where I had purchased my ticket and explained my situation. The man at the counter informed me that he could do nothing. "Matters of this kind are handled through our Chicago office," he explained.

"But, sir," I answered, "I need the money today."

He scowled, "Yes, and I could have sold your cabin a dozen times if I had known this."

At my insistent pleading, the clerk finally agreed to speak to the manager in my behalf. In a few moments he returned with my money. I shouted, "Hallelujah!" and promptly purchased a ticket to the "bottom of the world" on another steamship line.

Two days later I was walking up the gangplank of a steamer bound for Australia. Dr. Craig, founder of Glad Tidings Temple and Bible Institute of San Francisco, and his students, came to see me off. As the great ship RMS *Makura* slowly pushed away from the dock, breaking the brightly colored streamers, I felt that I too was breaking away from the only world I knew. The night was majestic and the starry city of God was above us as we passed the famous Alcatraz Prison, and passed under the Golden Gate. No mission society or church was sending me. I had only the call of God on my soul, the vision in my heart, and twelve dollars in my pocket. There was nothing to fear.

4

Twenty-one days after sailing from San Francisco harbor, with stops in Tahiti and Rarotonga, our ship pulled into the port at Wellington, New Zealand, for a thirty-six-hour stopover. I did not know that Howard Carter was at that moment in the mountainous interior of New Zealand teaching at a ministers' retreat.

While praying a day earlier, Howard Carter had asked God, "Where is the young man that was supposed to meet me in California and never came? I have lost him."

The Lord spoke to him that I was on a boat then pulling into the harbor at Wellington. He wrote a note to me saying, "Go on to Australia and minister until I arrive. We will travel from Sydney together."

Mr. Carter asked one of the ministers, "Would you go home for me? I will have a friend there tomorrow from America and I would like you to give this note to him."

That next morning at eight o'clock, I left the boat and began looking for a Full Gospel church. By eleven o'clock I had found Baptist, Methodist, Church of England, Salvation Army, Presbyterian, but could not find anybody who knew anything about a Full Gospel church. Finally I stopped a stranger on the street and asked him, "Is there any church in this town where the people say 'Hallelujah' or 'Praise the Lord' in church?''

He replied, ''Yes, I think so,'' and pointed across a railroad track and up a little hill in the distance. I followed his directions and found a small Assembly of God church and parsonage. My knock at the door was answered by a towering man who looked down on my slight frame (I was still not much more than a hundred pounds.)

I started to introduce myself, ''You don't know who I am, but. . .''

''Yes, I do,'' he interrupted. ''You're Lester Sumrall.''

I nearly fainted. ''I've never written to anybody in this country. How could you know who I am?''

''Howard Carter told me you were coming.''

A moment earlier I had nearly fainted. Now I nearly ran. This Howard Carter was so spiritual he was spooky. I wasn't sure I wanted to be around a man like that at all. I thanked the pastor and after a time of fellowship with him boarded the ship. The next day I sailed on to Australia alone.

Two days later, at four-thirty in the morning, I awoke to peer out the porthole at the glimmering lights of the God-designed harbor of Sydney. It was dotted with islets, each with its own flashing to warn passing mariners.

As the ship pulled into the harbor we were boarded by the pilot, state doctor, and emigration officers who met us in a motorlaunch. All passengers were given declaration forms to fill out, with questions regarding nationality, occupation, etc. One of the questions was, ''How much money have you?'' Underneath this question it read, ''If you are a foreigner staying in Australia three months, you must have two hundred pounds.''

Two hundred pounds! The twelve dollars in my pocket

were worth less than three British pounds. I left the space blank and went before the immigration officer.

Just ahead of me in line was a young American and I could overhear the conversation between them.

"Seventy-five dollars!" The officer bellowed indignantly.

"Yes, sir, that is all."

"We don't want beggars in Australia; we want tourists with money."

"I'm sorry, sir. That is all I have."

"Then give me your passport and ticket," the officer demanded. "We are going to put you on the next boat back to America."

Now it was my turn to meet the officer. Reticently I handed him my declaration and he glanced over it.

"An American, eh?"

"Yes, free born."

"A minister, huh?"

"Yes, of the Christian religion."

"Say, there is one question you have not answered," and taking his fountain pen he said, "I will fill it in for you. How much money have you?"

"Well, I don't have very much," I stuttered.

The officer looked up and barked impatiently, "I didn't ask you that question. How much money do you have?"

"Well," I hesitated, "I really do not have very much." Then mustering the best smile I could under the circumstances, I added softly, "My present reserve is a bit short, sir."

"Where are you going from here?"

An anointing came upon me as I answered, "I am going around the world to preach the gospel to those who have never accepted Christ as their Savior. I am going to Java,

Singapore, China, Manchuria, Korea, Japan, and I know the Lord will provide."

With that the officer went to fetch the chief inspector. I stood and prayed silently.

When the inspector arrived he asked the same questions and once again I gave the same answers. While I held my breath he looked at me for a moment in silence and said simply, "We are going to let you land."

The following day at noon I met Mr. Greenwood, pastor of Richmond Temple in Melbourne, who invited me to preach a few nights at his church. The welcome from the Melbourne Christians was hearty, but they gave me no pay for my ministry. The last night of the meeting, Pastor Greenwood said, "It must be wonderful to be rich like you Americans."

"Yes," I responded, "it must be wonderful." As Mr. Carter and I had agreed, I gave no hint of my need.

Going back to my room I cried much of the night. The next day I was scheduled to go to Bendigo, a city about one hundred miles away, and I had no money for a ticket. I prayed definitely for God to give me five pounds. Afterwards, the first man I met said that he and his wife felt impressed while in prayer to give me a gift. He stuck a sealed white envelope into my hand. Back in my room I hurried to open it and with tears of thanksgiving to God I counted out five crisp one pound notes.

After preaching in a few of the Full Gospel churches in Australia, some of the pastors challenged me. "When you evangelists come from America, all you want is to minister in our larger churches. Why don't you go and raise us up a church?"

They had challenged the right man. That was the thing I knew how to do best.

I rented a tent, called it the "Canvas Tabernacle," and set it up in Brisbane, capital city of Queensland. From the first night souls found God at the old-time altar, in the old-time way. What had worked in Arkansas and Mississippi and Tennessee I found worked just as well "down under."

One problem that plagued our meeting in Brisbane, which had not been a problem in the United States, was the bitter opposition from the Communists. They came and stood outside the tent almost every night. If I preached on world conditions, and especially Russia, they would nearly go wild with rage. One night while they were heckling outside the tent I exhorted my congregation, "If you talk about the devil, his children get angry." That night they stopped their heckling and went home.

Several miraculous healings also accompanied that crusade in Brisbane. One young lady came for prayer for a cancerous sore that had completely eaten through her nostril to the outside of her nose. When she removed the cotton which covered her sore it was a terrifying sight. She said that a doctor was going to operate on it.

I said, "Let the Great Physician do the operating. He does not use knives." We prayed for her and in a few nights she was back testifying of her miraculous healing.

The tent was near a tavern and one night I had to physically throw out two drunks who were disturbing the service. They were sitting in the back of the tent making fun of me, God, America, and everything else. I took them by the nape of the neck and the seat of the pants and shoved them out into the night, ordering them not to come back until they were sober.

One night near the close of the six-week campaign, the service was interrupted by a young man who rushed onto the platform. His face was white and he appeared to be in great anguish. At first I thought he wanted to fight, but when I saw the tears start to flow I knew he was under deep conviction of sin. He knelt and prayed until God's peace erased the anguish of his soul. I then asked him to share what God had done in his heart. "Last night," he testified, "I was so angry I was going to burn down this tent, but a power I have never felt kept me from doing it. Praise God, now I am saved!"

At the end of six weeks, when we took down the tent, there was a congregation of about three hundred converts. The new church had to send to England to find a pastor and a Full Gospel lighthouse was established in Brisbane. That work has gone on to become a great church.

I spent Christmas that year with Pastor Duncan of Jubilee Temple in Sydney. During the next few days we held special meetings with the gracious outpourings of God's blessing, climaxed by a watch night service on New Year's Eve.

On the first day of 1935, at 10:30 A.M., I anxiously watched the beautiful white S.S. *Maraposa* as she gracefully steamed into the harbor at Sydney and docked at her wharf.

With homesick eyes I scanned the ship's crowded deck for Howard Carter, but in vain. Then in the customs shed, I finally came face to face with Brother Carter. I was so happy to see him that I yelled and gave him a hearty hug. It had been five months since the Lord had so marvelously brought us together. I had not seen him since. In the next few years Howard Carter would become closer to me than my own father. He would have the most profound effect upon my life of any person other than my mother.

Sometimes together, sometimes separately, we continued

to minister throughout Australia wherever God opened the doors. Perhaps the crowning achievement of our ministry on the Australian continent was the establishment of a Bible school in Queensland for the preparation of young Australians for the ministry. An efficient staff of teachers were secured and the principal, Mr. Wiggins, came from England to take charge of the school.

On March 9th, at 9:30 P.M. the gangplank was lifted and a harbor tugboat gently pulled the SS *Morella* away from her mooring. As Howard Carter and I waved farewell from the deck, our Australian brothers and sisters sang ''God Be With You 'Til We Meet Again.'' The ship moved slowly down the Brisbane River and into the Coral Sea. Our destination was Java, fifteen days away.

When the *Morella* threw her steel hawsers to the dock of the East Indian port of Surabaja, for the first time we were facing the Oriental in his homeland. For the next two months we were to travel the length and breadth of this England-sized island which claims to be the most densely populated section of the planet.

We were met by Mr. and Mrs. Van Abkonde, who were to be our hosts on this torrid, humid island of perpetual summer.

In the evening our friends called to take us to our first meeting in Java. Arriving at the church we found a large concrete auditorium which seated about twelve hundred people. There must have been at least two thousand people present with hundreds standing in the aisles and around the wall. As we entered, the Javanese choir was singing the ''Hallelujah Chorus.'' ''Hallelujah'' was the one word of their language we understood. Brother Carter spoke first through an interpreter and then I was asked to give an evangelistic message. When I faced that cosmopolitan congregation, I saw the faces of Malaysians, Javanese, Dutch, Chinese, and English. To my amazement many of these faces looked familiar as if I had seen them before. But I had just arrived, traveling many weeks by ship to get to this backside of the world. I thought, "They've never been away from home and you've never been here before." And suddenly I knew—it was the vision! I had seen them in the vision!

And did I ever get busy preaching. And did I ever preach my heart out. These were the people to whom I had been sent! When the appeal was given, a great number came forward to be saved. As all the different races knelt at one altar, praying to one God, I saw that the ground was level at Calvary.

From Surabaja we preached in the cities of Blabok, Semarang, Solo, Madiun, Kediri, Probolinggo, Malang, Temanggoeng, Djokjakarta, and several others. Everywhere we went we were warmly received. In many cities the crowds so overflowed the mission halls that the meetings were moved to a masonic temple or theater building. Our main difficulty was the curse of Babel, the language barrier. Our interpreters, being Dutch, did not always understand our English idioms. At times they would say, "Vot brudder, vot you say, brudder?" Despite our difficulties, God's word did not return to Him void. The gospel net dragged in the fish from the vast sea of souls.

Java was very much a land of contrasts. We were invited to visit the fabulous one-mile square palace of the Javanese Sultan, Amanggku Buwano, whose name means, "He who has the world's axis on his knees." From this ornate "city within the city" of Djokjakarta, we drove two hundred miles till there was no more road to travel. Then we walked a winding trail all day long into the mountainous region to the primitive village of Gambang Walla, many miles from the nearest sign of civilization. Here in a bamboo tabernacle with an earthen floor, we preached to the smiling brown-faced villagers. Our messages were translated from English to Dutch to Javanese.

Here a blind woman, the oldest person in the village, asked to pray for us. What a prayer that poor peasant woman uttered! With her head nearly touching the ground, she seemed to rock the heavens. Our interpreter could not explain it all for weeping, but said that she was praying for God to richly bless our visit to her village. That prayer was worth the day-long journey by foot over the mountains.

After crisscrossing the Island of Java for 3,000 miles, ministering daily, we continued our journey to the Asian nation of Singapore. We stayed in this island city only two nights, but we saw many souls saved at special meetings in the mission hall.

Boarding the S.S. *Terukuna Maru* we sailed next through the South China Sea to the crown colony of Hong Kong. To our surprise we were met at the dock in Hong Kong by two of Brother Carter's former Bible school students who were now missionaries to Yunnan Province.

Our ten days in Hong Kong were feverishly busy with three meetings daily. In the first service at 9:00 A.M., Brother Carter led a Bible study for the benefit of the English-speaking missionaries. A general meeting was conducted at 11:00 A.M., and an evangelistic service in the evening. Every service was crowned with souls being saved and the sick being healed. On the final evening, a large number of people were baptized in water by immersion in an impressive service.

From Hong Kong we desired to travel some three thousand miles to the borders of Burma and Tibet, but our funds were not nearly enough for the fare. On the night before we were to buy our tickets, the native church gave us an unexpected love offering which came to $260. Also, a number of Chinese Christians brought canned foods for us to take inland. These gifts saved our lives.

After a stormy trip across the Gulf of Tonkin in a small combination steamer, we landed in the muddy bay of Haiphong, French Indo-China. The next morning we boarded a little mountain train for a three day journey into Yunnan Province, the most backward section of China.

As the railroad is dangerous, and the mountains very high, the train does not travel at night. At dusk, passengers, train, and all just stop over until the next morning. After crossing the border into mainland China at Laokay, the route became one of the most remarkable feats of engineering in the world. For the first time in my life I became travel sick as the little French train swung us through about three hundred tunnels which pierced the towering peaks of China's mountains. The curves were so sharp that you could look out of the window and see the rear coaches entering a tunnel you had just come out of. On emerging from each tunnel the carriage was full of smoke and cinders as there were no screens on the windows and it was too hot to have them closed.

At five o'clock on the afternoon of the third day, our train finally pulled into the station at Kunming, the capital city of the great Province of Yunnan, southwest China.

From the station we rode in a rickshaw through the huge gates of the walled city, with guards standing overhead, guns in hand. We gazed in wonder at the quaint hieroglyphics and carvings in the magnificent architecture of this old city.

Our initiation into the cruelties which were taking place in China came within our first ten minutes in the capital. We passed a group of men who were stoning another man to death. He screamed and groaned as large stones tore his body. The crowd looked on and laughed. Someone said that he was a thief.

For two weeks we stayed in the city. In the mornings we had conferences with the missionaries who had gathered from across the province for a time of fellowship and spiritual refreshing. In the evenings the missionary would blow his trumpet in front of the large mission hall, and in five or ten minutes it would be filled with Chinese. A wooden partition was built down the center of the church to separate the men from the women while worshiping.

After a hymn and prayer, the speaker began. The people would listen intently for some five minutes, then in a grand stampede, two-thirds of them would get up and walk out, leaving you stammering in the pulpit. Mr. Carter and I developed some drastic gymnastics to keep the people entertained while speaking, but even this failed sometimes.

From Kunming we felt it God's will to visit the far inland mission stations. The British and American consuls both advised against this journey as the route was infested with robber bands and Communists. These would be glad to capture us for ransom, or they might choose to sever our heads from our shoulders, as they had done to missionaries John and Betty Stam a few weeks earlier. At that very moment a Mr. Bosshardt of the China Inland Mission was being held for ransom somewhere in this section.

Also, the missionaries said it was the ''wet season'' and

no one travels for a long distance unless it was very necessary, since the rains wash away horse roads and even villages in a very short time.

Still, we felt it to be the Lord's will for us to go. When we walked through the west gate of Kunming, followed by a mule caravan of fifteen animals, we bid adieu to the last ramparts of civilization for nine long weeks. The British consulate sent a guard of soldiers with us for protection. Our destination—the borders of Tibet and Burma.

Outside the city we got astride our mules (mine was named Henry) and followed a narrow, slippery, rocky path. We journeyed through deep rock ravines, over narrow ledges at dazzling heights, into the "Switzerland of China."

In almost every muddy little village along the way we would have precious fellowship with missionaries from different countries—Germany, Holland, Scandinavia, Australia, and others. The barriers of denominationalism and nationalism were torn down completely in these remote outposts. Everybody offered us hospitality in their compounds and ministry in their churches.

When friends asked us what it was like preaching to the natives inland, I told them I thought our sermons had three effects on the congregation. They were moving, soothing, and satisfying. Moving, because as we began to speak the people moved out the door. Soothing, because those who stayed usually went to sleep. Satisfying, because we never saw the same congregation twice.

One morning our caravan walked slowly out of a village where we had spent the night with five or six other caravans. I was sitting on Henry reading the *Reader's Digest* as he plodded down the trail. It must have been an hour later that I looked up to realize I was lost. I could not see a white person anywhere on the trail. I looked at the Chinese, but did not recognize any of them. They laughed at me when they saw my bewilderment. We rode on for another hour hoping vainly to see a familiar face. I came to the conclusion that I must be on the wrong road. Here I was, fifteen hundred miles from Hong Kong, and lost. I could not speak a word of Chinese, and not a penny was in my pocket.

Now Henry sensed we were lost. He threw his head back and began to bellow. It was awful! Henry's regular gait was three miles per hour, but now he broke loose and ran. I was bouncing on his back, holding on for dear life, and yelling, "Whoa, Henry, whoa!" But he was a Chinese mule and couldn't understand my command. Soon we were not with any caravan.

Rounding a bend in the mountain path I prayed, "Lord, please show me the way to go." There was a fork in the trail and I breathed a prayer as I took the left-hand turn.

Fifteen minutes later I met a man who began to jabber something to us in Chinese. I signaled that I did not understand. He then grabbed Henry by the head, turned him around, and gave him a good kick in the behind. I held on as Henry took off again in a gallop. An hour later, on the other side of the mountain, we found our caravan which had stopped for lunch. They wondered where I had been—and so did I.

My diary for July 31st records, "Tonight we are sleeping in a barn nearly full of opium poppies. They are the seed for next year's sowing." We saw many people—from a five-year-old boy to an old man—smoking this dreadful poppy juice which benumbs the faculties and saps all the vitality from the system.

Twenty-nine days after leaving Kunming, our caravan

finally arrived at Chu-tien. This area was part of Tibet until the Chinese pushed them further into the mountains. When I met these square-jawed Tibetans, I had the uncanny feeling that these were people I had seen before. And then I realized again that I recognized them from my vision of a world going to hell. With great compassion I shared with them the good news of Jesus Christ.

From Chu-tien we turned southwest climbing the lofty, rugged, wild mountains to 13,500 feet, and after two days traveling we arrived in Wei-hsi. Here we spoke to the people of the Lisu tribe near Burma. They were a rough, primitive people with coarse features and homespun clothing. An astonishing work had been done with them. Hundreds had been converted to Christianity. When the Lisu come to church, they start greeting you a great distance away, and as they came nearer, you could hear them "Wha whaa" in their own tongue, meaning "Peace to you." This greeting echoed from the hills over and over again. I found it exciting!

Traveling four days south from Wei-hsi over the endless mountains, we came to Lan-p'ing. Here we stood on a high peak and viewed beautiful tropical Burma. As the rain had fallen and the roads were gone, we had to have a special guide direct us. Dangerous streams had to be forded and twice we had to repair the road before the mules could pass safely. Where the narrow road had caved into a deep ravine we had to cut the mountain away, making a path for the animals.

Just one of many experiences will give more of an idea of our living conditions. One day at noon we came to a small village and stopped at the "cafe" for lunch. As we walked into the room, the thick smoke choked us and burned our eyes. The table had a cloth on it made of layers of spilled food, soot, grease, etc. We looked to one side and saw the cook, naked all but for a loincloth, standing by his brick furnace that had no chimney. He had a large iron pot on the furnace where everything was cooked. On one side of us was a dog and on the other a pig. The floor was earthen.

We noticed that the cook had a rag tied around his head. This was used for cleaning out the cooking pot. The dog got in his way so he hit him with the rag and wiped the perspiration off his body. As our dinner was cooking, he walked over to the door for some fresh air and used this same cloth for a handkerchief. When the food was ready to eat, he reached for some bowls, wiped them out with the same rag and put our food in them. Yes, we ate it. We were *really* hungry!

There were times when our lives held no premium. We were having dinner one day at a place where two men had just been murdered. This frightened our soldiers so that we had to dismiss them and finish our trip without any natural protection. We passed places where once thriving cities had been burned to the ground by the Communists, with the loss of many lives. A number of days we were warned not to travel as the road was infested with robbers, but we traveled every day, except one, and then it was the rain that stopped us.

At one time we passed a spot where the Chinese said the Reds had killed twenty-five men only hours before, and we were traveling in that direction. God protected us and we did not see them.

Another morning, high on a mountain summit, we turned a sharp curve around a huge boulder and there we saw three filthy, ragged men with cruel, scowling faces, sitting, polishing their long, shining rifles.

Without uttering a word the three men joined our caravan, walking behind us. The Chinese horsemen, who usually joked all the time, were silent and pale as death. We walked five minutes, ten minutes, fifteen, with those guns just behind us. One of the men finally spoke, "We want money."

Our interpreter gave him what he asked for, then the bandit put his hands to his mouth and screamed. The whole mountain resounded with his voice. On the next ridge came an answer, then the ragged trio walked away. God brought us through a desperate, ungoverned, bandit-ridden land, in peace.

Three months to the day after sailing for Hong Kong, we steamed back into the beautiful harbor again, viewing Victoria Peak, the green Gibraltar of British domain. Our next destination was Canton, the sprawling metropolis of South China, a city with a recorded history of 4,000 years.

From Canton, we traveled inland again to Fatshan for a week-long meeting. Later we ministered in Shanghai and then on north to Tientsin.

In every place God blessed our efforts with the healing of many souls and bodies. Mr. Baltau, the pastor in Tientsin, said there were 105 who definitely decided for Christ in our week's visit there. Many others who had been seeking the infilling of the Holy Ghost found their fulfillment.

From Peking, the national capital, we traveled north by train to Kalgan on the Mongolian border for ten days of special meetings. This was an unusual city to labor in as the powers of darkness were desperately fighting to hold their victims. But the kingdom of darkness was no match for God's power and many souls were saved and delivered from Satan's power.

We were privileged to stand on the Great Wall of China

and look right into the dark mystical land of Mongolia. We beheld the very places where battles raged between the primitive Mongols and the crafty Chinese 500 years before the herald angels announced the glad tidings of Emmanuel.

For our final mission in China we returned to Peking, the great imperial city of North China. Here we held three services daily, dividing our time between American, British, and Swedish missions.

During these many months in China it was apparent that permanent trouble was brewing in the East. The far inland missionaries were having to evacuate their mission stations as the Communists were taking over the territory. The Japanese army at the same time had already captured North China, and we watched as the Japanese soldiers looted the banks of China taking the silver and gold from the vaults. We rode in trains loaded with this gold and silver headed for Japan. As we turned our attention toward Japan, we did not know that we were witnessing the beginning of a second world war. Nor did we realize that soon all doors for evangelism in China would be closed.

In our visit to the Land of the Rising Sun we began meetings in Tokyo and worked our way south. Our first meetings were in the Takinogawa Church Bible School. Mr. Carter lectured to the Bible school students during the day and I preached in the evening services. Mostly missionaries and Japanese Christians attended the meetings, but the few unconverted who did attend were convicted of their sins and accepted Christ. Several of those who were already converted were filled with the Holy Spirit.

My personal opinion of Japan, after visiting her largest cities, and also small towns, was that the so-called Christian nations had given Japan a western civilization, had brought her from medieval obscurity into the global limelight, but had miserably failed in giving her Christianity. I found Japan with all her enlightenment and progress to be one of the most difficult fields for successful soulwinning.

Our acceptance as foreigners was no doubt greatly affected by the war talk in all the newspapers. Japan was siding with Hitler and getting ready to make her gigantic push into Asia. Americans were not very popular in Japan, but the Christians were openhearted and kind to us..

Eight weeks and two days passed swiftly as we ministered in the churches of this island empire of the East. Although the results were not spectacular, we were encouraged to see scores of Japanese born into the kingdom of God.

Across the deep blue waters of the Inland Sea we next made our way to Korea, Land of the Morning Calm. In the capital city of Seoul, we were met at the station by two of Mr. Carter's former Bible school students from England. It was a great pleasure to speak three times daily to the Korean audience, as they sat still and listened intently.

One night in a meeting I said, "Now I will tell you a story," and my Korean interpreter said, "Now I will tell you a lie." A missionary very kindly helped me through this awkward situation. During our brief stay in Japanese-occupied Korea, several healings took place. A man lame for four years was healed and another man, mentally deranged for two years, was restored. These and other healings strengthened the faith of the saints and made sinners to see the power of Jesus Christ.

Manchuria, Japan's puppet state, was next on our itinerary. This is a large territory lying north of China, south of Siberia, with Korea on the east and Mongolia on the west.

In the city of Mukden we learned that many local

Christians had been imprisoned as anti-Japanese instigators. This made some people afraid to go to church. However, we had good attendance and God gave us a great time of revival and blessing. Many were saved and healed.

North of Mukden was Harbin, Manchuria's great cosmopolitan city. It was bitter cold when we arrived there and the river was frozen to a depth that large trucks were able to pass over the ice. We were shocked to see bodies of people lying along the street, frozen to death. Beggars had stolen their clothing while others had kicked them to one side to let the traffic pass. We asked why they were not taken up and were told, "Oh, they will be picked up next spring, put on carts, and taken outside the city and burned."

Beggar women, sometimes with a child in their arms, could be seen on the streets, two-thirds naked and shaking with cold and dying from hunger, screaming to the passers-by for a few pennies with which to buy opium. How my heart broke for these souls for whom Christ died.

While in Harbin we ministered at the Russian Eastern European Mission Station to a congregation of White Russians who had escaped the Communists. To look at this congregation was to behold expressions of grief and hardness of countenance that results from much trouble and privation. When preaching to them, however, we found tender hearts. About ten new converts wept their way to Calvary during our three services there.

This ended more than a year of ministry in the Orient. We left a people whose way of life was totally different than ours—where dessert comes first at the meal, where the masculine dress is of silk and women wear trousers, where the man shakes his own hand in introduction and his surname comes first. But my spirit knew that I would return again and again to these hungry lives seeking the Bread of Life.

Our next destination was Poland, to be reached by train across Siberia and Russia. For nine days we were on the train in the wilds of Siberia, where temperatures dipped to fifty below zero. From the train window we could occasionally see the weary, poorly dressed exiled workmen who easily could have been Christian brothers exiled for Christ's sake. A few hours stop in Moscow gave us the chance to see this Mecca of Socialism, the Jerusalem of Communism. Until we reached the Polish border town of Stolbce, we were constantly under surveillance by the secret police.

What a pleasure it was to minister to the eager, hungering souls we found in Poland. From one city or village to another we were welcomed by overflowing crowds in the mission halls and churches. Many had walked for days to hear the Word of God preached. Some had never seen a foreign minister. Whole villages would declare a holiday and come out to the services. This was particularly gratifying in a country that is over 85 percent Catholic.

After eight or ten hymns and a long prayer, usually three or four sermons were the order of the day. It was marvelous to see how these people worshiped God in such freedom of the Spirit. The Holy Ghost descended and Pentecost was repeated time and again.

When I asked one pastor where all the visiting people found lodging he said that about one hundred slept on the floor of the mission hall, with only a bit of straw under them. They had walked as far as sixty-five miles in snow, some of them wearing shoes made from strips of bark from willow trees, and stockings made from rags wrapped around their legs. As long as their souls caught a spark from off the heavenly altar, they did not worry about cold weather, black bread, or a bed.

Our five-and-one half weeks of Polish ministry was perhaps the hardest and most tiring itinerary of our tour, but it was also one of continual blessing. Over a hundred miles by springless wagon, sitting on a little bag of hay, food beyond digestion, or infestations of lice, meant nothing compared to the blessings we witnessed that God poured out on His children.

Crossing the Polish border into the German Reich, we were now in the heart of the European continent. One ride through Berlin and the tremendous intensity of life and speed of a western nation could be felt and seen. Two-thirds of the men and boys we saw meeting on the street gave each other the Nazi salute of raised open hand with curved thumb. The greeting was "Heil Hitler!" The sign of the swastika was everywhere.

Semitic hatred was rampant. Signs could be seen in many public places, "No Jews Allowed;" "Through these gates does not lead to Palestine;" "No dogs allowed," etc.

We were not at liberty to preach in different churches in Germany or Berlin. A special permit for each church had to be granted by the chief of police. The Gestapo often sat in the meetings and took notes on the sermon. It was noticeable to us that when a strange person entered the hall, the German Christians watched him nervously and a depressing feeling filled the church.

Our sermons were restricted. The interpreter had forewarned us not to speak in strained tones, or lift our voices unnecessarily. He also asked us not to preach about divine healing or on the Holy Spirit, as the Nazis think these things fanatical and would close the church.

The difficulties of worshiping in Nazi Germany made the faith seem all the dearer. The fellowship with the saints in Germany was precious. We were saddened to learn that shortly after our visit most of the churches were closed by Hitler and padlocked in his mad fight to place all churches under his direct supervision.

The final leg of our tour took us into Scandinavia, the glorious land of the Midnight Sun. Mr. Carter and I were invited to conduct special meetings at Oslo in the great Filadelfia Temple (Church of Brotherly Love) which was the largest in Norway. Thousands packed this tremendous church with hundreds of people standing on the outside. God gave great grace to the services there, and in Stockholm, Copenhagen, Amsterdam, Rotterdam, and other cities as well. Everywhere we preached the Lord confirmed His Word with signs following.

While in Holland, Mr. Carter had an attack of malaria and we canceled our engagements in Belgium, France, and Switzerland, flying directly to London, having circumnavigated the globe. Mr. Carter made the comment, ''We started with nothing, we return with nothing, and we desire nothing but the privilege of proclaiming the glad news that 'Hallelujah, our Lord God Omnipotent Reigneth!' ''
For over two years we had averaged traveling a thousand miles a week through thirty countries and the islands of the sea. We had preached in eighteen foreign languages with the help of sixty-five interpreters. Yet my insatiable desire to reach the lost masses of the world had only increased.

Standing in the White Russian railway station in Moscow, I remembered reading a local newspaper written in English. A young Communist leader had stated in an article, ''We young Communists of Russia will live for Communism and we will die for Communism!'' That rash declaration sent a wave of holy indignation over my being. I could do no less for Christ. I knew that my journey had just begun!

5

Three months after that first missionary tour with Howard Carter ended in London, we sailed back to the shores of America in 1936. It had been two-and-one-half years since I had started on my round-the-world trip. It seemed longer.

First, Brother Carter and I came into Toronto, Canada, to speak at a national conference. From there we made our separate ways down into the United States. I ministered at churches in New York, Washington, D.C., and Philadelphia, and then into the South where I was able to visit with my parents. Next I traveled into the Midwest, up to Chicago, and over to South Bend, Indiana, for speaking engagements. The revival in South Bend was a particularly blessed one, although initially I was not impressed with the city itself. The meetings, which were first scheduled at the South Bend Gospel Tabernacle for a weekend with Pastor Thomas Zimmerman, continued for several weeks. This meeting brought many invitations for others. Little did I know that this fair city in America's heartland would later become my home.

During these few months of evangelistic work in the United States, my heart was very restless. I yearned to get back to the heathen on foreign soil and that opportunity wasn't long in materializing.

Howard Carter flew down to Brazil for a special Bible conference and I followed a few days later by ship. There we teamed up and ministered throughout this largest of the South American countries. We carried the message to the great cities and then penetrated the hinterland, all the way to the wild tropical borders of Bolivia.

After several months in Brazil we sailed back into war-torn Europe, preaching first in Portugal and then in England, France, Switzerland and Holland.

Ministering to the French people was particularly gratifying on this tour. In these days, just before the Second World War hit, we saw a tremendous move of God from one end of France to the other. We spent several weeks itinerating the new churches throughout France that had been raised up by an Englishman named Douglas Scott.

The people of this predominantly Catholic land seemed to have a greater than usual faith. They would claim and receive healing for just about anything we would pray for.

We found the superstitions of the French sometimes perturbing. One night a lady came to the meeting, got all excited, accepted Jesus as her Savior, and asked for a Bible. When she came into the church the next night she announced enthusiastically, "It worked!"

"What worked?" I asked.

"The book you gave me."

"Why, did you read it all night?"

"No," she said. "I put it in the mailbox all night and it kept the devils out of my house."

I explained to her that the book is powerful when you read it and it gets inside of you, not when you stick it in the mailbox.

While in Europe, we made our headquarters at the

Hampstead Bible Institute in London. I traveled in crusades, teaching at the Bible school between meetings. Howard Carter, as president of the college, asked me to lecture on evangelism.

In England I pioneered three new churches. Without denominational backing I would rent a hall and conduct a crusade assisted by a talented young man who directed the music. We would advertise the crusades by distributing handbills and placing ads in the local newspapers. These meetings were blessed with marvelous conversions and healings.

My American preaching style was not always received by the staid English. After preaching a few nights in one rented hall in a London suburb, I was approached by a dear little old English lady. "You know, Mr. Sumrall," she stated, "God is not deaf. You are yelling too loudly!"

I leaned over and put my hand on her shoulder and replied tenderly, "Yes, sister, and did you know that God is not nervous either."

In 1939, Europe was neither a safe place to live in nor minister in, as the chariots of war were racing furiously across the continent.

Throughout the two years that I lived in and out of London the British intelligence would occasionally knock at my door and ask, "How are you getting along?" Then they would ask me to show them American money to prove that I wasn't without funds. Now as the war was intensifying I was notified by British authorities that Americans with temporary visas should prepare to leave. A personal visit by the British police finally made it clear; I had no choice but to return to America. Howard Carter, being a British citizen, stayed with the Bible school. I took a freight ship from Holland across the Atlantic to the United States. On this exciting trip I was the only passenger and had the run of the ship.

For about six months I preached in churches across America. But, as before, the call to world evangelism would not let me go.

I was in a special missionary service in South Bend, Indiana, and heard a missionary to Alaska speak. His tale was one of the most pitiful I had ever heard. He talked about how difficult the work was in Alaska, saying that he had spent most of his life there and it was the hardest place in the world to win souls. The challenge gripped me when he said it was impossible to get an evangelist to visit Alaska. After the service he told me to my face that evangelists were afraid to come to that far northern territory where drunkenness and debauchery were rampant. True to my nature, that was a challenge I couldn't pass up.

"I'll come," I told the missionary. And I went, spending the entire winter season in Alaska, from fall to late spring. It was my joy to preach in nearly every town in this great land. I spoke in the high schools, lectured in the University of Alaska, and preached as far north as Wiseman, seventy miles north of the Arctic Circle, and as far west as Nome, on the Bering Sea.

During that long arctic winter I was used of the Lord to raise up new churches in Ketchikan, Fairbanks, and Anchorage. All three of these are still good churches today. As in England, I was not subsidized in this work. However, through the freewill offerings of the people, God more than supplied the need.

Just as I arrived back into the States, the doomsday news came that the Japanese had attacked Pearl Harbor. The nation was thrown suddenly and violently into the Second World War. As a concerned citizen I rushed down to the navy enlistment office and volunteered my services as a chaplain.

The sergeant across the the desk looked through my credentials then looked up at me and said, "After reading what you have been doing, if I were you I would just keep on doing it. We have plenty of men to fill our quota of chaplains."

If I thought he was telling me that I was doing too much good to change my missionary work, he soon shattered that. "The kind of men we want as chaplains," the sergeant added, "are not evangelistic types like you. You will just run into a lot of problems in the chaplaincy."

I thanked the sergeant kindly, walked out, repacked my bags, and headed south of the border for what would turn out to be a two-year extended missionary-evangelism tour through Latin America.

The world was at war but I seemed lost from off the face of the earth. I lived in the cities and jungles of Central and South America, journeying from Mexico to Argentina, not missing one country. I traveled by mule back, canoe, freight truck, and every other means imaginable. In one primitive area I did not sleep in a bed for several months but slept in jungle hammocks, on floors, or wherever I could find a smooth spot to lay down. It was thrilling and gratifying to see thousands of people healed, both soul and body. Some of my experiences and observations of this tour are recorded in my book, *Through Blood and Fire in Latin America.* I dedicated this book to the forty Christian denominations in which I ministered.

Our southern neighbors marshaled themselves before me in a fascinating variety of colors and cultures. As I wandered through their streets and plazas I had ambivalent feelings—one moment the scene resembled China, and the next moment, Java or France. A touch of every other part of the earth contributed to making the kaleidoscope which is Latin America.

The world understands and can analyze the religion of India, China, or Africa, but comprehending the religion of Latin America is more difficult. Contrary to what I had been led to believe, the Catholic church did not have a monopoly on the people there.

In the vast Gran Chaco of Argentina and Paraguay, the heart of South America, I ministered to many tribes of the original men of this continent. They are indeed "forgotten men," having been neglected by governments, charities, and most religious communions. Their plight is shared by their brother tribes from the once mighty Aztecs of Mexico to the Onas and Techuelches of Patagonia. I have never been confronted with more dire poverty and depressing human hopelessness than while visiting the remote privitive villages of these indigenous peoples of Latin America. They comprise an estimated three hundred fifty-six known tribes, many of them existing in a state of cannibalism and savagery.

The Spanish found the Incas living in houses of granite; I found them living in houses of mud. Once this proud race wore golden ornaments, but I saw them wearing brass, copper, and alloys. This tragic economic deterioration of the red man has been brought about by his white "superiors," and much of it in the name of Christianity.

I was shocked to hear people say that the Indians do not possess souls, therefore it is useless to attempt to evangelize them. Many believe, as did the Spanish theologian Sepulveda, who maintained that "As the Indians were not mentioned in the Holy Scriptures they do not belong to the human race, and for that reason can be legitimately used by Christians for private ends."

Agusto Schiambari, the Indian chief of Gran Pajonal, mentioned that the priests still take Indian children (against the will of the parents) and sell them into homes in the cities as "permanent" servants.

Because of these abuses, to ask an Indian of the Gran Chaco to become a Christian is to insult him. He regards all white men as "Christiano" and he an Indian. To him, becoming a Christian would be asking him to hate his own people. Therefore, I learned that the only successful approach was to teach them of a world Savior whose name is Jesus Christ, and ask them to become "believers."

Most of the civilized tribes are Catholic in name, but I found that in reality they have a dual religion. This peculiar brand of Latin American Romanism incorporates many of the Indian's ancient pagan beliefs. In Chichicastanango, some of the nationals told me, "We pray to the Virgin and if she does not answer, we go to the witch doctor, who communes with the gods of our fathers and he answers our prayers."

Drunkenness was common among the Indians. I saw them often during the holy feast days, lying in the church doorways so intoxicated that they could not stand. In Huancayo, Peru, I observed an Indian funeral where every man and woman present was drunk. While some lay on the ground completely intoxicated, others tried to push dirt over the coffin. They had no religious rites because no priest wanted to be bothered. My heart ached as I witnessed throwing their dead into a hole without a word or a song.

During this very time that I was ministering across Central and South America, many influential churchmen in the United States were advocating the removal of all Protestant missionaries from Latin America as part of the Good Neighbor Policy. I found that intelligent people in Latin America were horrified by the North American's lack of knowledge regarding their true religious beliefs.

In one small town in Central America, the commandante (equivalent to our chief of police) was eager to grant permission for a series of evangelistic meetings. It happened that he was angry with the local priest who had created a lottery and raffled off the virtue of the Virgin Mary. The lucky ticket had been drawn by chance by a local prostitute. Although she was now the proud possessor of the virtue of the Holy Virgin, she continued to operate her house of ill fame.

In many cities of both Central and South America I noticed that there were small images representing the child Jesus displayed in the Catholic churches. These images were reported to have come into existence by miraculous means. Typical of these was the "Holy Child of Atocho" in Santa Ana, El Salvador. The image has blue eyes, is dressed in clothing similar to that worn by a modern priest, is fat like a monk, and yet is supposed to be a Jew. The priests say that the little image fell from heaven. The child images are constantly presented with costly gifts from many devoted but misled worshipers.

One of the things hardest for me to accept in Latin America was the common use of sacred names. I met many people named Jesus, both men and women. When I met Senor Don Espiritu Santo (Mr. Holy Spirit) I thought his name to be a sacrilege in the christening process. I was horrified at the ultimate blasphemy of a saloon named "Sangre de Jesus " (Blood of Jesus).

It was impossible not to notice the ringing of the church bells in Latin America. The people were taught by the priests that the slow mournful pealing of the bells for funerals is of spiritual significance and helps the dead. However, I was impressed that for some funerals the bells rang only a few times while at others they pealed for several hours. I was informed that there was a charge of ten cents for each time the bell was rung. If a person had no money the bell would not toll for him at all.

In some parts of Latin America the local priests tried to keep the people away from our meetings by telling them that the evangelicals buy human souls for money and that the people who attend their meetings have sold their souls to them. God even turned this around for His glory. Poor people came and asked how much the missionary would pay for their souls, making a wonderful opportunity to give the simple gospel of Christ to those in great darkness.

Occultism was another religion embraced by a large number of Latin Americans. While stepping from a taxi in Bucaramanga, Colombia, returning from a youth meeting at the local Presbyterian mission, the taxi driver proudly announced, ''I have North American religion, too!'' He enthusiastically took from his pocket some literature from the United States and showed it to the missionary and me. The front cover read, ''From the Rosacrucians in San Jose.'' We lost no time in explaining to the taxi driver that this was not North American Christianity. We presented him with a New Testament, which he gladly received.

This was one of numerous brushes with occultism which deeply stirred my soul. The growth of esoteric systems of spiritism, theosophy, Rosacrucianism, I Am, metaphysics, etc., throughout Central and South America, is alarming. In one town of about one hundred thousand in Brazil, I saw ten or fifteen spiritist centers on the main streets. Someone informed me that there were sixty-three in the city altogether. Most of these spiritists also belong to the Catholic church, making religion even more confusing. There were liberal Catholic churches where seances were permitted in the church.

As I ministered the gospel in this complex and bewildering religious confusion, I realized that the answer was not to plant Protestantism as just another cult in Latin America. Rather I longed to see the person of Jesus planted in the hearts of the people. Often while preaching before large congregations throughout Latin America I declared that I had not come to convert the people to Protestantism, but to Jesus Christ. I was made to realize afresh that the world does not need another religion, but the only Savior and Redeemer.

6

It was at a wedding in the great South American metropolis of Buenos Aires, Argentina. The setting was a typically Latin patio with sun streaming through the luxuriant foliage overhead. Golden shafts in the green dappled the cool, flowered mosaic of the patio floor.

Among the many women who were busily decorating the tables for the wedding dinner, one striking young lady caught my immediate interest. I asked a missionary friend to introduce us. She was Miss Louise Layman, a charming young missionary from Canada. I was enchanted by her sweet smile and gracious manner from the moment I first saw her.

"So this is Louise Layman," I mused. I had heard of her before. Back in the autumn of 1940, enroute to Alaska, I had conducted a week of special meetings in Prince Rupert, British Columbia. The pastor there had informed me that on the same day that I sailed north for Alaska, a missionary from South America, a Miss Layman, arrived on a boat from the south to give talks on the Argentine. We had missed meeting each other by a few hours. Upon the return trip from Alaska I preached in several Canadian churches and in each town the Christians spoke of the missionary from the Argentine and of the rich blessing she had been to them.

She had ministered where only the most courageous and zealous dared go. I admired her before I knew her.

On my missionary tour of Latin America once again my curiosity about Louise Layman was aroused. In the lovely city of Mendoza, Argentina, in the home of a missionary, I heard how she had come up from Buenos Aires and labored with these people for six months. These friends declared that her life had brought golden sunshine into their home and great blessing to their mission.

Now, across a wedding table, we finally met.

A vivid recollection of that fateful day is of a brief moment as Louise was playing the bridal march on the electric organ. It happened as the bride marched in and stood beside her groom at the altar. I looked up toward Louise; she looked back, and we both smiled. That's all. But something churned way down inside me. We later teased each other as to who smiled first, but we both knew it was simultaneous.

The next time I saw Louise was in Henderson, seven hours by train from Buenos Aires. It was at eight o'clock on Christmas Day that my interpreter, Mr. Sorensen, and I arrived at the local mission station. I was surprised to find a gaily wrapped parcel under the family Christmas tree with my name on it. My surprise turned to mild embarrassment when I opened the gift to find that it was a little wooden donkey with wheels under his feet. Louise had given me my first gift. I christened the donkey "Luisa" (Louise in Spanish). A few days later, while in the home of a missionary with a small child, I gave the burro away.

From Argentina I traveled up the La Plata and Paraguay rivers to Asuncion, Paraguay. Several days on horseback then took me to the Church of England mission among the

Legua-Moscoy Indians of the Gran Chaco Boreal. On this long journey I wrote a letter to Miss Layman, thanking her for the donkey and telling her of giving it to the child. Upon returning to Asuncion I found a rather indignant letter from Louise regarding the donkey affair.

I wrote back to apologize and she answered to say I was forgiven. Then I wrote to say "Thanks" and she wrote to say "You are welcome." Thus for better than a year we continued to correspond. Eventually I proposed marriage to Louise and she accepted, all by mail.

Wednesday, February 15, 1944, was the second greatest day of my life. The greatest day was when at the age of seventeen I decided to follow Jesus. The second day in importance was my thirty-first birthday, when I asked Miss Layman to be my wife.

I had returned to the United States from the two-year tour to Central and South America and was preaching a series of meetings in Minnesota when I finally decided to send the letter of proposal. Day and night for weeks I had sought God to be certain of His will in the matter. I had also sought the advice of several Christian people whom I respected.

When I wrote the letter of proposal my brain was whirling and my heart was beating fast. The first letter did not satisfy me, so I rewrote it. The second draft sounded too formal so I rewrote it again. That afternoon I stuck an airmail stamp on the final draft, sealed it with a prayer and a kiss, and sent it on the wings of the wind to far-off Argentina.

Thirty-one days later, March 18, 1944, the postman delivered Louise's answer. That day I made this entry in my diary:

"I am engaged today! One month and three days after

Lester Sumrall as a teenage evangelist.

Lester Sumrall in Tibet on mule back.

Lester Sumrall sitting next to Howard Carter at a Bible Conference in Poland in 1936.

Early evangelistic crusade.

Lester & Louise Sumrall on their
wedding day, as they began their
50,000 mile missionary honeymoon.

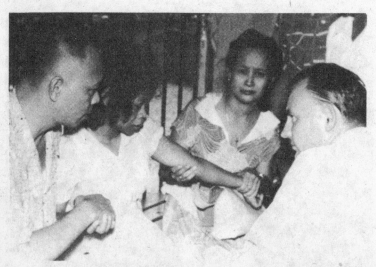

The deliverance of Clarita Villanueva brought revival to the Philippines.

The Sumralls greeted by children from their first orphanage in Baguio, Philippines.

At the ground breaking in 1968 of WHME Radio Station in South Bend, Indiana.

In 1972 we began broadcasting in our first television studio at WHMB TV-40 in Indianapolis, Indiana.

In June 1985 we moved into our new headquarters and church,
Christian Center Cathedral of Praise in South Bend, Indiana.

Dr. Lester Sumrall speaks in New Life Temple, Hong Kong, one of the churches he founded.

On Christmas Day 1985, Lester Sumrall read scripture on WHRI Shortwave, one of the most powerful outreaches of LeSEA Ministries.

At the dedication service in April 1986 of Bethel Temple, Cathedral of Praise, in Manila, Philippines.

Lester Sumrall spoke to 25,000 cell group leaders in Central Full Gospel Church, Seoul, Korea.

I wrote my proposal, the answer was received. Sitting here in the great Pan American air terminal in Mexico City, waiting for the plane to take me to Tuxpan where I shall go back and visit the Otomi Indians, I read again the letter received this morning from Louise, forwarded to me from my home in Chicago. She has consented to leave the Argentine and return home to Canada where we shall be married later this year. May God unite our lives to do a great work for Him in every part of the world. She said she had prayed about the matter for a week and had consulted her senior missionaries on the field—that is a good spirit. The long string is about to knot! My heart feels certain she will make a fine companion as she is the choice of God, and my choice. The distance is so great and the war restrictions and censorships so slow, it takes time for word to come and go. I trust the same censor read both letters and knows how it all came out.''

Louise had three months to prepare for departure from Argentina. When the long-awaited day arrived that I was to meet her at the glittering international airport at New Orleans, her plane did not arrive. The following evening at seven her name appeared on the passenger list. Even then the immigration authorities would not release her until some American stood responsible for her crossing the States and entering Canada. I was more than glad to take Louise off the immigration authorities' hands. We embraced, and I whisked her away in my green Hudson coupe.

After Louise arrived home in London, Ontario, my Hudson became quite well known in the district. I was traveling to various cities in both Michigan and Ontario during those months of May to September. Every possible chance I headed for London and my beloved Louise.

These were days of romance, dreams, planning for the future and making memories. It was a time of synchronizing two personalities, of blending two lives toward a harmonious whole. We were amazed to learn how our ideas and ideals ran parallel. Never have I known of two lives so alike to be so miraculously led in separate ways until ultimately united to labor for the Lord.

Our birth dates were only eleven days apart; both had accepted Christ as teenagers and promptly given our lives to the Christian ministry; both felt a call to foreign missionary work; both had first departed for the mission field on the same month of the same year. On September 30, 1944, at the age of thirty-one, the two of us became one.

It was a beautiful ''Indian summer'' afternoon, a perfect day for a wedding. At exactly 2:30 P.M. I stood facing the altar at attention as the organ played the familiar strains of Lohengrin. My pulse quickened and my breath drew short as the vision of loveliness that was Louise seemed to float down the white-carpeted aisle on the arm of her stepfather, Rev. J. D. Saunders. My brother, Rev. Ernest Sumrall, pastor of the Stone Church, Chicago, was best man. Officiating was Dr. Wortman, missionary physician and uncle of the bride.

At the close of the ceremony, Mrs. Wortman sang ''Together With Him.'' The last verse of the song was especially prophetic of the life we would live together:

Together with Jesus, constrained by His love,
We seek for the lost ones and point them above.
From valleys of service to mountains of rest
He guides us and keeps us; in Him we are blest.

Our union was pronounced; the wedding supper was ended; and farewells were said. Our Hudson roared away across the twilight of the Ontario countryside, rich in its autumn colors, toward Niagara Falls. Four hours later we arrived at the honeymoon cottage which we had reserved overlooking the world famous cataracts. But our honeymoon would not end at Niagara Falls. It would be extended into a fifty thousand mile missionary journey that would lead us throughout the Americas, literally from top to bottom and back.

Like the Apostle Paul on his missionary journeys, we had no predetermined itinerary planned. We set out to minister in as many countries as the Lord would direct, and the doors of ministry were miraculously opened before us. Travel was extremely difficult during those years when the world was at war, but time and again the invisible hand of God made the way for us when humanly speaking there was no way.

After leaving the majestic waterfalls of Niagara, where we spent several pleasant days, the first service of our united ministry was at a Thanksgiving youth rally in the Canadian metropolis of Toronto. Next we conducted a week of special meetings in Montreal, capital of Quebec and the citadel of French culture in North America. We preached through an interpreter to the French-Canadians whose lively meetings reminded me forcefully of earlier visits to France.

From Montreal we boarded a train for a long wearying journey through the provinces of Quebec and New Brunswick, to the Peninsula of Nova Scotia. We had been told that the Maritime Provinces had been largely neglected by the evangelists. This challenge compelled us to enter Nova Scotia to conduct crusade meetings. We found this province to be backward and primitive by the standards of the great interior cities of Canada. Our itinerary formed a circular route around the peninsula where we ministered in a dozen cities and towns. We did not witness the sweeping revivals among these conservative residents of Nova Scotia that we would later see in Latin America, but the Lord graciously blessed and a number accepted the saving grace of Jesus Christ.

Our experiences in the town of Lockport were typical of the simple life style we shared with the people of Nova Scotia. We lived with a poor family in the rural section where we slept in the front room on an improvised bed. The house heater was in this room. In the mornings it became my responsibility to arise early and make a fire in the old wood stove. Then we tidied up the room for the family to use as a sitting room during the day. Meals were served in the kitchen near the heat of the wood range and we washed in a basin of water near the table. Although they were poor in material goods, the hospitality we received from this kind family, and others like them, was honest and unembellished. We enjoyed it.

The weeks passed quickly, our work in Nova Scotia soon ended, and Louise and I arrived back in the United States in time for a great New Year's youth rally in Detroit. But we were back in the United States only to make preparations for the southern portion of our honeymoon journey. Our hearts and minds were set toward Latin America.

Our application for a passport to travel in Central America and the West Indies was refused on the grounds of international disturbances. Puerto Rico and the Virgin Islands were American possessions and no passport would be needed to visit there. However, we ran into another difficulty. The army would not permit North American women to enter Puerto Rico during the war unless they had professional reasons. We petitioned the army chief and within ten days Louise was granted entry into Puerto Rico.

Light was bursting over the Atlantic horizon as our

Douglas DC-3, a twenty-one seater, skirted Biscayne Bay and the city of Miami and headed across the straits of Florida toward the sparkling Caribbean Sea. By 2:30 P.M., after a short stop in Port-au-Prince, Haiti, we landed in San Juan, the capital of Puerto Rico. It didn't seem possible that we were 1,000 miles from Miami, Florida.

We were pleasantly surprised in San Juan by a great welcome meeting which was arranged for our first night on the island. Pastors from various parts of the island were present along with the entire student body and faculty of Mizpah Bible School. It was a grand meeting and at the close, when I gave the appeal, eight souls came forward for salvation. It seemed to be God's seal of blessing upon this part of our missionary venture.

The churches of Puerto Rico we found to be strong and indigenous, governed and propagated by nationals. We had a religious liberty here that is absent in much of Latin America.

In various cities we applied for and readily secured permission to use the city plaza for a public meeting. In each place hundreds listened to the gospel over the loudspeakers. There was no heckling and few disturbances. While I was preaching in San Juan one night five drunken men disrupted the meeting. Police arrived and promptly took them to prison. The penalty for disturbing public worship was six months in jail or $500 fine, or both. The law was strictly enforced.

Some of our most enduring memories in Puerto Rico were made the day we accepted the invitation to visit a jungle wedding. We were informed the walk from the road terminal to the jungle church was only two kilometers and that we could wear our good clothes. We learned otherwise—the hard way.

Our party trudged slowly into the tropical jungles. The trail was just a narrow path up the almost perpendicular sides of the mountain. Coffee and bananas grew in abundance on the steep mountain slopes. Oftentimes a gorge, hundreds of feet deep, was only a slip of the foot away. The trail was studded with sharp slippery rocks which caused us to stumble often.

The worst part of the climb was the heat of the terrific tropical sun. We became drenched with perspiration. My belt became watersoaked, faded, and discolored my clothes. My coat clung to me like a shapeless wet rag. Louise had been told to wear a pair of white shoes—which she ruined that day.

We walked until noon, having started at nine. The entire group was exhausted and some insisted on stopping to rest when the guide admitted that he was really lost. When the group heard this some grumbled while others wept. On the trail through the dense wilderness we had seen no one. We had not seen half a dozen huts even on distant hillsides. As we turned to start down a slope, we experienced a tropical downpour of rain. The wet red earth was as slippery as soap but not nearly so clean. Several times we had to cross mountain streams. Like Gideon's band, we refreshed our weary dehydrated bodies with a few handfuls scooped up as we crossed.

It was past two-thirty in the afternoon when we found a small cottage on the side of the mountain where a family of Christians welcomed us. These good people insisted that we borrow some of their clothing while ours dried. Then we laid down to rest and these folk served us fried eggs and fried bananas—in bed.

While we rested, the farmer took his ancient shotgun and, with perfect aim, wounded a chicken. Spry as a boy, he then jumped over a precipice and caught the flopping fowl which he butchered and we ate.

At six-thirty we decided to try to make it to the wedding. We learned that the church was now just three hills away. We slipped and slid and climbed, arriving too late for the wedding supper but in time for the ceremony. We were filthy with red and orange colored mud. Our bodies were becoming sore and cold from the damp clothing in the high mountains.

The meeting began with everyone praying heartily in unison, including the bride and groom. The officiating minister then announced a hymn and the congregation began to sing in Spanish, "Yes, our Lord is coming back to earth again. . ." Then they sang "How Firm a Foundation," followed by another prayer in concert.

Next, the pastor announced he had brought a visitor with him who had traveled around the world, and that he was sure the visitor would be glad to preach a sermon for them. While the people listened intently and patiently, I spoke about the marriage of the Lamb of God and His bride, the church. Louise interpreted for me.

After the message, the pastor announced he would perform the ceremony. In the flickering light of a kerosene lamp he read the ritual and then proceeded to give a personal talk to the young couple. In plain language he told the young man that he was to be faithful to his new bride. Then he lectured the girl that she must serve her husband and take care of her home. Finally, he admonished the young people in the congregation that if they were seriously in love it was best to marry as quickly as possible, thereby giving no place to Satan.

The ceremony closed with another prayer and the large

crowd marched out in a long procession. They filed down a mountain path by the light of *mechones,* a bottle filled with oil with a rag protruding from the top. It was after midnight when the late dinner was ended at the bride's home. The newlyweds bade farewell, then set out into the night. Ahead of them was a two-hour walk over a series of muddy hills to a small cottage that had been prepared by the groom.

After a short night of sleep we were up at dawn the next day to start our trek back across the mountains toward civilization. Our feet were so blistered we could hardly limp. Yet we made it back to Ponce in plenty of time for a preaching engagement that night.

The most distressing time during our 50,000-mile honeymoon came after visiting the Santurce Franquito in Puerto Rico. Here we were both bitten by contaminated mosquitoes and Louise contracted malignant malaria. Her fever shot up to over a hundred and three. The fever abated for a few days and then came a second attack, worse than the first. I was quite concerned for my bride so I went to consult an American-educated doctor. After hearing my description of her symptoms he offered little hope, saying that she would perhaps be dead before morning. I was scheduled to preach that night. Even though my wife was at the point of death I felt that my obligation to win the lost came first. I left Louise with some nationals and went to my appointment. As the old bus jogged into the country toward the church that evening I sat and wept. My interpreter sitting beside me wept. At every turn of the road the devil seemed to say to me, "You will bury your wife on this island." As I prayed, faith welled up inside me and I answered the devil half aloud, "Satan, you are a liar. My wife will live. She will be healed tonight!"

At the revival crusade I told the congregation what the doctor had told me earlier that day. These simple trusting saints of God prayed for Louise and together we claimed her healing.

After the meeting I rushed back to her and knelt beside her bed. As I prayed the fever miraculously left! She was completely healed that night. Though we traveled on through the West Indies and South America, up the Amazon River for 1,100 miles where there are millions of mosquitoes, there was no recurrence of malaria.

Invitations came from missionaries in the Virgin Islands who had heard of our revival mission. Feeling it God's will for us to continue our journey in that direction, we bought airline tickets to St. Croix, the largest island in the Virgin group, made up of fifty islets and cays.

Life in the Virgin Islands seemed to us a dream world. Everything was quiet, peaceful, and slow. The natives, 90 percent of African descent, lolled around as if there were no work to do. The people were ultra-friendly—almost too much so. As we walked down the streets of St. Croix small groups would congregate and discuss us among themselves. When we passed they would stop us and say, "Hello, what is your name? Where are you from? Do you like our island?"

We took the plane back to St. Thomas island where we were asked to preach in a mission. When the meeting began there were only three natives and the two of us present. The native pastor led the meeting as if the house were full. As I spoke the tiny congregation backed me up with "Yeah; at'right; amen; sure." Before the sermon was ended I had a congregation of a dozen who gathered and listened from the doorway. I addressed most of my remarks to them.

During this time we were trying to find passage across the Caribbean quarter-moon to Trinidad. Pan American Airways put us on their waiting list but said that it would take months before tickets would be available. Even then we would stand a high chance of losing our seats to military personnel unless we possessed high priority. Shipping agencies were no more encouraging than the airlines.

One day almost by accident, we found a Dutch cargo boat, the *Prince Bernhard.* This small freighter plied between Dutch Guiana and Puerto Rico during the war because it could not return home to Holland. The captain said he would be happy to drop us off in Trinidad on his return trip from Dutch Guiana after he unloaded a cargo of cement from Puerto Rico. The Edward Millers, another missionary couple enroute to Uruguay, sailed with us. We paid one of the crew members to relinquish his bunk room to our lady folk. Edward and I purchased army cots and slept in the galley. While hundreds were stranded in Puerto Rico with no means of getting away, the Lord opened a way for His servants to continue to Trinidad.

The boat made stops en route at two of the Windward Islands, St. Lucia and Grenada. In Grenada we were able to preach twice at a native church to a house full of eager hungry souls. Within a week of leaving Puerto Rico, on a torrid August morning, we anchored in the flat, humid harbor of Port-of-Spain, Trinidad. We were now only ten degrees north of the Equator. Trinidad is separated from Venezuela, South America, by the Gulf of Paria, seven miles across.

The ship gave its signals of arrival and hoisted its flags asking for medical, customs, and immigration clearance. After two steaming, suffocating hours, the native officials dressed in smart, white suits climbed aboard and issued us permits to land.

A walk down the main street in rustic shabby Port-of-Spain was almost like a walk around the world. It is a strange cauldron of Orient, Occident, and Africa boiled together. There was every shade of the racial spectrum. The Hindus and Mohammedans had their temples and many of the Africans and others still practiced their black magic on this supposedly Christian island.

Our schedule in Trinidad was full. On the very afternoon we arrived I spoke over the radio-diffusion. I was then the speaker for services in the church that night. In Port-of-Spain, the Prince's Building, the largest auditorium on the island, was obtained for a special campaign. A great number accepted Christ at these meetings. We then continued our ministry to the smaller towns.

In Tunapuna, the Panphilian High School auditorium was secured. In Arouca we preached in the Presbyterian church. At the great Waller Field Air Base, it was the "Paint Room," where men found new life. Here Louise and I celebrated our first wedding anniversary. The missionaries and soldiers gave me a stuffed crocodile and my wife a beautiful tray made of varicolored inlaid wood. It was not one year since we began married life together, and we had just completed the north half of our 50,000-mile missionary honeymoon.

Flying south toward the huge sub-continent of South America, our Pan American plane crossed the equator to Belem, Brazil. We were in the capital of the rich tropical state of Para, ninety miles up the Amazon from the Atlantic Ocean. In this metropolis of the Amazon we spoke for Rev. Nels Nelson, a Swedish-born missionary. In his tremendous church of 3,700 baptized members we enjoyed large crowds and an enthusiastic reception to the gospel. Pastor Nelson kept a record of 140 persons who accepted Christ during our ten days of special meetings.

Plans were developed for a flight up the Amazon, the world's widest and deepest river. This was a fulfillment of a desire I had had for many years. Our plane was the *Baby Clipper,* an eleven-seater seaplane. Five hours after departing Belem, we were in Manaos. It was sweltering hot as we went ashore. A welcomed tropical cloudburst gave us a good soaking ten minutes after our arrival.

Manaos was a decaying city. The war had ended and this boomtown was now deserted by American soldiers and Brazilian rubber pickers. We preached in two missions there, and in both places it was not easy. My wife and I estimated that 90 percent of the people were undernourished and victims of malaria. Many of them seemed to be doped and could not participate wholeheartedly in the services. Also the heat was so oppressive that it sapped our strength. Nonetheless, we saw a dozen or more make decisions for Christ. We were especially grateful for one young soldier who stood up during the message one evening and announced, ''I want this Christ right now.'' I ended my sermon immediately and led him to Calvary.

On October 31st, we boarded the *S.S. Virginia,* a ''Good Neighbor'' ship formerly used on the Mississippi, for our return down the Amazon. In good Latin American style, our ship sailed seven days late and there was nothing we could do but impatiently wait.

Our companions on board ship included pigs, ducks, chickens, turkeys, a dozen cows, two monkeys, a parrot, a dog, several cats, many large turtles used for food, and fish. Most of these shared the third-class accommodations with many humans. The passengers hung their hammocks above the animals unperturbed. We were fortunate enough to book firstclass tickets through the kindness of a Baptist friend. In our cabin we roasted by day and steamed by night.

Being warned not to drink the water on the boat (a friend had contracted typhoid fever that way) we treated the muddy waters of the Amazon with Halazone water purification tablets. Our menu of rice and beans was supplemented by "beef on the hoof" which was brought on board. As we floated downstream at twelve miles per hour, we watched the men kill a cow, cut her up, and carry the pieces to the kitchen. The bread served on the ship was rank, but the chef sold better bread—which we bought.

Stopping at six ports of call we took on more cattle. Men on the *Virginia* screamed and pushed to get them into an improvised pen. One cow was injured in the process and left to die on the lower deck. Passengers slept in hammocks hung between stalls of cattle. Piles of crude rubber, vegetables, fruit, and other goods were also loaded onto the already crowded boat.

It was Sunday when we finally arrived back in Belem. Our mission into the interior of Amazonas was completed. We would now travel southward.

Our itinerary took us to crusades in the Brazilian cities of Bahia, Rio de Janeiro, Sao Paulo, and Belo Horizonte. We continued south through Uruguay to Argentina. It was here in Buenos Aires where my wife and I had first met. Now we had returned on our honeymoon missionary tour. Rev. Jeffery had prepared union meetings in the Y.M.C.A. auditorium. These meetings were greatly blessed of God. We also preached in La Plata and then down to where my wife had formerly ministered in Henderson, Argentina.

Over the majestic snow-capped Andes from Argentina, we flew a Pan American World Airways plane to a meeting in Santiago, capital of the boot string republic of Chile. This was a union meeting of all evangelicals and was conducted in a Presbyterian church. The meetings were pregnant with a spirit of revival. Anywhere from ten to fifty unconverted persons made decisions for Christ in each service. It was beautiful to see all denominations cooperating harmoniously as one body. The Union Evangelical Choir was made up of some fourteen Protestant groups.

A great help in the meetings was Theodore R. Bueno, my interpreter. He seemed to share my anointing as I preached, reproducing inflections and emotions that struck direct to the hearts of the Chileans.

Saying farewell to our friends in Chile, we departed Santiago at 6:30 in the morning by plane for Peru. This was my third visit to Peru for meetings, the first for Louise. This time it was Easter. Our union meeting was held in the First Methodist Church, largest church auditorium in Lima at the time.

One of the things that impressed us most about being in Peru during the Easter season was the unusual parades. The Romanists carried statues which depicted Mary as alive and Christ as dead. But in our services among the evangelicals, Mary was dead and Christ was alive. Our hearts were overjoyed to see the large church auditorium packed to overflowing, and many standing night after night. Many found the living Savior during those meetings.

One of those converted was Alejandro Pickman, a young Peruvian of twenty-three. The seed of the gospel had first been planted in Alejandro's heart at an open-air meeting in the plaza of his town of Chilca. He listened to the entire service but did not understand the Christian terms used. He did not know how a man could speak of religious things without wearing clerical attire. Alejandro had read a Bible that was given to him as a lad, and he was curious to understand it better.

Like many ambitious young Peruvians, Alejandro wanted to live in the capital city of Lima. There he accepted a job as a domestic in a wealthy home. One day while sweeping the floor he found a printed announcement of an open-air meeting conducted by a Catholic woman. He went to the meeting only to hear a tirade against the Protestants. So crude and rude was the woman's agitation that it angered Alejandro. Something stirred up inside him and he boldly interrupted the meeting by declaring to the woman, "I have visited thirty-three Catholic churches in this city to pray and my heart is not satisfied. I have decided to become an evangelical."

That evening Alejandro sat in the second bench at the union meeting and heard me preach by means of an interpreter. "How does this American know my life? Why, he has never met me, yet every word he speaks is directed right to my heart," he mused.

When the moment of decision arrived, I asked those who desired Christ as personal Savior to stand. Alejandro was one of the first to his feet. With a large group of others he left the crowded auditorium and went into the prayer room for instructions. There he confessed his sins; he confessed his Savior. He now understood the meaning of being "born again."

Alejandro grew steadily in Christ from that moment. Shortly he became secretary of the Rimac Church, a downtown church in Lima. At his own expense, he and a

Christian friend made a three-month gospel tour in which they spoke in fifty towns and in seventeen public schools. The Lord was with them as they sowed the seed of the gospel in the byways of Peru. The last I heard of Alejandro he was making preparations to enter Bible school and become a full-time minister of the gospel.

This was fulfillment of my main purpose. My goal was not just to win the few souls I could reach, but to plant the indigenous church and help to see it become a healthy national organism bringing Christ to the nations.

The time for Louise and I to return for a while to America had now come. Leaving the airport in Peru at 7:30 A.M., we arrived in New Orleans that night, making stops in Panama and Guatemala. In Guatemala we deplaned long enough to rush over to a local church and speak a few moments before returning to the airport.

When our plane nosed out over the Gulf of Mexico, darkness covered the earth and we lolled back in the reclining seat for a short nap. But we could not sleep; we were too excited. Our great honeymoon adventure was ending. We were both sad and happy. Our bodies were weary. According to my wife's carefully kept records we had ministered in twenty countries and islands touching approximately one hundred cities and towns. More than two thousand souls had responded to our invitation to accept Christ as their Savior.

It had also been a time of spiritual growth and maturity for the two of us. We had read the entire Bible through together in our private devotions, beginning with the first page and ending with the last ''Amen.''

The blackness of the night was penetrated by the dazzling lights of New Orleans. As the plane bounced onto the runway of the airport we didn't know whether to laugh or cry. It had been over a year since we left this same airport for Miami and on to the West Indies. Now we were home. The first chapter of our adventure together had ended, but the greatest adventures of our life were yet ahead of us.

7

The war had ended while my new bride and I were on our 50,000 mile honeymoon journey. The world was quickly returning to normal.

We had been in the city of Ponce, Puerto Rico, when the radio announced that the Japanese had surrendered to the United States. Within minutes of the announcement the streets were jammed with people screaming, shouting, waving flags, and rejoicing. There was a tremendous sound of horns and sirens and bells. Many ran to the churches and filled the altars with exuberant prayers of thanksgiving to God for peace.

We had continued our tour and by the time we arrived back in the United States the war had been over for about a year. Louise and I were expecting our first baby and needed a place to call "home." We bought a little house in Springfield, Missouri, which became our headquarters for the next several months as we continued to speak throughout America at conventions, camp meetings, and missionary engagements. Our first child, Frank, was born in Springfield on December 31, 1946.

After preaching in several cities throughout the United States the opportunity came for me to travel once again to

Europe to minister among the ruin and rubble of that war-scarred continent. I left Louise and our new baby in Springfield where we had many friends. Taking the *S.S. Queen Mary,* I sailed for Southhampton, England. Immediately after arriving in Great Britain, I went up to London to see the churches and to minister in the places where I had been before. I was saddened to see where a bomb had scored a direct hit on Hampstead Bible Institute, effectively destroying it. Howard Carter had escaped physical injury, but the emotional stress on him during the war had been almost overwhelming.

It was shocking to see once beautiful buildings now reduced to bricks and rubble. Where large trees and lovely homes had been there was now nothing but scalped earth. Viewing such sights gave me a strange and dreadful feeling. I learned to hate war.

The people seemed dazed. The once mighty British Empire was disintegrating. You would hear people say, ''You mean we have to be fed by America? You mean the great British Empire can no longer take care of herself?'' Many Britishers were stunned that they had come out of the war bankrupt and there was not sufficient food and clothing to meet their needs.

We took the night boat across from Dover, England, to France. I revisited a number of the churches and pastors where I had been before in more prosperous times. In Normandy I wept to see the beach where our fighting men had landed—and so many perished. It was a scarred and devastated scene. Entire towns had been erased from the face of the earth. I realized that Americans who have seen war only in movies can't really comprehend its awfulness.

Much of the food available was very bad. In France I ate poisoned bread that was made of something other than pure wheat and I almost died.

From France I went by train across Switzerland into Italy. I was delighted to preach to weary souls throughout many of the cities of Europe. However, the most significant thing that happened on this tour was the work God began in my own heart. It was during this time that God began to urge upon me His plan for evangelizing entire nations in these troubled times.

I returned to America aboard the *S.S. Queen Elizabeth,* which gave me time to meditate upon the exciting plan that God was revealing to me.

God showed me that in most of the countries of the world a revival in the capital city could reach and influence the entire nation. In many of the smaller nations the capital is the center of political, educational, economic, social, and religious life. A great move of God in the capital with the establishing of a large center of evangelism could change the spiritual climate of a nation.

As I traveled from land to land I had seen every kind of missionary work under the sun. What I had seen at the same time excited and disturbed me. As I went from place to place I said, "Lord, we are losing this game; we're losing the battle." My heart was broken. I would think of pastors at home who were so occupied with one little place and I thought, "If Paul had been like these men, he would have gotten Jerusalem saved but the rest of the world would have gone to hell."

I had been in Shanghai, China, in a little church that seated about fifty people. They didn't need that many seats because they had only thirteen people present. Outside of that little place—the front room of a dwelling used as a church—were six million Chinese souls. I can't tell you how that tormented me. I would walk down the streets with a prayer in my heart and on my lips: "Lord, there are six million Chinese in one city. How are we going to reach them?"

There was so much spiritual intrigue in overseas operations. I saw many of the cities of the world left virtually untouched. When I went through Central America, there wasn't a single church of our denomination, not one, in any capital of the six republics.

Talking to missionaries and to missions boards I would say, "Brethren, why don't you go to the great cities? That's where the people are. What are you doing out behind the banana tree?"

They would reply, "Why, brother, it costs too much; we can't go." I boiled on the inside like a volcano when I heard that lame excuse. I thought, "I would go! I would pawn my suit or my suitcase, but I would go to the capital city."

One large Full Gospel organization had missionaries in the Philippines for twenty-five years. Every one of those missionaries had gone through Manila, the capital city, but none stopped. They went into little villages and towns, some remote places, and the great throbbing heart of the nation was untouched. Manila takes care of 75 percent of the total commerce of the whole nation—one city alone holds the whole nation in its hands—and they hadn't stopped to raise up a church. Some responded, "It's not missionary work in the large city. It's only missionary work in the jungle where you wrestle tigers and kill snakes." I didn't like tigers and I didn't care for snakes, but the cry of the major cities tore my heart day and night.

The Lord showed me three things about reaching the nations:

1. He showed me that much of the missionary strivings are almost futile, because we didn't bind the powers of the devil operating in the land. There is a compelling need on

the mission field to shackle the powers of Satan and set the people free. Jesus said to first bind the strong man, then take a prey.

2. Then after the people are set free from Satan's power, the minister or evangelist or missionary must not run off and leave the new converts. So often in our times when God gave a great revival on the mission field, the evangelist would quickly move on. As a result most of the revival was lost, for the new converts had not been settled in God's Word. When God gives a man two or three sons, he doesn't run away from them. He buys a house and provides for their shelter and care. We've got to do the same in the spiritual realm. When God gives a great move of His Spirit we must preserve the fruits of the revival.

3. There is simply no other way to take the nations for Christ except to go into the capital cities, the heart or the core of the nation, and erect evangelistic centers. Get the people saved and delivered and then they will go back to their own villages and win their kinsmen to Christ.

I spoke of this to mission boards, in conventions, and churches across America, but it mostly fell upon deaf ears and unbelieving hearts.

The Lord impressed me that I must demonstrate this plan personally. As I had never been a pastor I felt that I needed experience here at home first. Out of a dozen invitations to pastor churches in different American cities, God placed the city of South Bend, Indiana, upon my heart as a trial ground for this deliverance venture. South Bend was not a strong Protestant center. The churches of the city had not sponsored a unified revival effort since Billy Sunday's time. Most of the evangelical churches were struggling to grow. The Lord said that in this unlikely place He would show me how His work could be done quickly and victoriously.

I was conducting a revival in Memphis, Tennessee, when

the call came from South Bend. I had conducted successful revival crusades there several times in the past at the South Bend Gospel Tabernacle. When the church had been without a pastor on previous occasions they had invited me to come, but I had declined. To be truthful I didn't particularly like the city of South Bend. When they called this time I refused as before saying, "If I wanted to pastor a church I wouldn't go to that little town."

The following night the people in South Bend called me again in Memphis. They said, "We have fasted and prayed all day and voted again. You got 100 percent of the vote so evidently you are the one to come."

I said, "Well, that's very interesting. I appreciate that very much, but I can't come. God bless you," and hung up the phone.

On the third night another call came from South Bend. "The Lord told us that you haven't prayed about our invitation."

I remonstrated, "But I told you I wasn't coming."

"You are supposed to pray about it," they replied.

"Well, then I will pray."

I did begin to pray about South Bend and as I did the Lord revealed to me that this was to be my training ground for accomplishing the burden He had placed on my heart. I called back the good folk at South Bend and told them to give me six weeks to close out the meetings I had scheduled and I would be there.

It was early December when my wife and I and our baby son, Frank, arrived at our first pastorate. The South Bend Gospel Tabernacle was one of the most miserable little buildings you ever saw. When you stood on the side of the auditorium your head would reach the ceiling. It was about six feet high. The building had been put together with secondhand lumber and free labor during the depression. There were forty adults present in the Bible class my first Sunday morning. There were about one hundred children in the other classes.

The mandate of the people in asking me to come be their pastor burgeoned my boldness in leading the South Bend congregation. I told them, "If you want me here, then you will have to follow me. Otherwise I will leave." When spring came I sold their building and bought a large tent. We moved the office and everything into the tent. That was all the church we had.

For eleven weeks we held evangelistic services. I preached every night for the first nine weeks myself, then called in an evangelist to help me. God singularly blessed this venture of faith. By the end of the summer we had three times more people than the church had when we arrived. During this time we bought a lot on the corner of Michigan and Ewing, one of the finest intersections of the city. God miraculously helped us to raise the $35,000 to pay for the lot. Without any money, and a congregation of mostly poor people, we began to build. It was amazing how God led us step by step and supplied the need as we followed His direction.

After eleven weeks of glorious revival in the tent, snow began to fall in northern Indiana. We rented a third floor dance hall from the Copp Music company downtown and held services there for several months. By the following spring the back part of our new church building was completed and we moved in. By the summer we were able to occupy our new auditorium that seated a thousand. We named the new church Calvary Temple.

Not more than two or three weeks after moving into our new building, Rex Humbard came walking into my office and said, "I need a meeting very badly. A crusade has been canceled and our family needs a place to minister."

I had known Rex since we were both teenage evangelists in Arkansas. Also, I had preached a revival for a Rev. Ott in Dallas, where Rex and his father and mother were serving at the time as assistant pastors. He was now traveling with his evangelistic team of thirteen, known as the Humbard Family. I told Rex, "Get them over here. We are ready for revival."

By the time the crusade had been going for a few nights we had more people than we knew how to handle. They were in the streets, inside, outside the building, and standing. We received about a hundred and fifty new members into the church during the meeting. Rex said, "I'll come back next summer with the tent." I said, "Okay," and the next summer we gained another hundred and fifty new members. Oral Roberts, Clifton Erickson, William Branham, and many other evangelists came to help us. The whole world began to hear about what God was doing at South Bend.

We rented city buses to bring people to Sunday school. The mayor of the city came out to see it and said, "This is the most fantastic thing in our city." As God helped us to capture the imagination of our city we grew to have one of the largest Sunday schools and churches in the nation at that time. We had over one hundred classes in our Sunday school and reached a high attendance of more than twenty-four hundred.

The church expanded so fast that we never stopped building. It seemed that every month we were adding another new addition onto the side or the back.

At the same time that we were building the work in South Bend, I continued to be involved in missionary work around the world. In 1950, I took a six-week missionary tour to Europe, Africa, the Orient, Israel, Egypt, and India. Charles Blair and Ernie Rebb accompanied me on this trip. In most places we would conduct three-day crusades. I generally spoke on the first night and let the other men speak on the following nights.

One of the highlights of this crusade was our city-wide crusade in Manila, Philippines. Paul Pipkin arranged the meeting for us at the Rizal Stadium. I had ministered in Hong Kong and Singapore on both sides of the Philippines, but this was my first visit to this country.

In the three-day crusade we saw hundreds respond to the gospel appeal. We also spoke in a number of churches in the area. We saw the awful marks of war. Most of the downtown government buildings still showed the signs of battle. Wrecked buildings were everywhere with weeds growing up around them. Manila was no longer the ''Pearl of the Orient.'' It was a city sad to look upon, a city with a scarred face and a broken spirit.

Returning to South Bend I once again lost myself in the challenge of the work there. In the next two years we consolidated the church and paid off its indebtedness. Also during this time we were blessed with the birth of our second son, Stephen, on June 27, 1950.

But the world harvest was never out of my mind. To further the cause of world evangelization we had conducted a highly successful missionary convention. The crowds had filled Calvary Temple and the offerings were greater than at any previous missionary convention. The Spirit of God rested beautifully on the people.

It was about three o'clock on the final Sunday afternoon of the convention and I was alone in my bedroom. As I relaxed for a few minutes before the evening service, God spoke to my heart. His words were not audible, but they were unmistakable. What He said would dramatically change the course and destiny of my life.

God said, "Will you go to Manila for me?"

"But Lord, the work is so great in South Bend now. You called me to this city and I have not finished my work here." I soon found myself arguing with the Lord. "Why not send someone else to Manila? I will stay here and raise money for missions and take missionary preaching tours."

God did not argue back, but His gentle voice persisted, "Will you go to Manila for me?"

One thing that had continued to drive me was that tormenting vision of a world going to hell. Every day it was the one predominating thought of my mind. When I was asleep I often dreamed about it. The vision would not let me go.

My heart was as heavy that afternoon as it had ever been in my life. Without further hesitation and from the depths of my inner being, I cried, "Lord, you know I am willing to go any place in the world as long as you go with me. Yes, I will go to Manila."

The Lord replied, "And I will do more for you than ever before." What a challenge! What a promise!

The burden lifted. Ecstasy flooded my soul like a river of heavenly blessing. The Spirit witnessed to my spirit that my decision was the will of God. Marching downstairs, I announced to my wife, "Darling, we are going to Manila! We are going to leave South Bend and raise up a work for God in the Philippines."

Louise smiled and half seriously asked, "When?"

"We are going as soon as we can get packed," I replied. Then I told her of God speaking to me in the bedroom. She knew that I was serious and assured me that she was ready to go with me.

When I first broke the news to my church board and congregation no one seemed to fully believe that God had really spoken to me about going to the Philippines. Some said that I was crazy to just walk away from one of the finest churches in the world to pioneer a work in the Orient. The people reluctantly accepted my resignation and elected another pastor to take my place at Calvary Temple.

As my family and I prepared to go, the call of Manila burned hot within my bosom. Before me was the challenge of one of the world's great cities.

Manila is an English-speaking city of several million people. At the time it was predominately Roman Catholic and rife with false religions and cults. There was not one aggressive Full Gospel church in the city.

Through the years I had learned some things about God's *modus operandi.* I knew that God works through men, calling a specific person for a specific task. In His omniscience and for His own purpose He had called me to Manila. I felt both honored and humbled by this pressure of divine destiny.

I also knew something about divine timing. God has His time for intervention in the affairs of men, for revival, for deliverance. I knew I must move with God in His time, otherwise the opportunity would be forever lost, the work would go undone.

To me this was no faint knock or timid rap at the door of opportunity. It was an incessant pounding that demanded my response, and the time was *now.*

8

The regular ocean liners were on strike in the summer of 1952. My family and I sailed from San Francisco on a Swedish freighter, the *S.S. Wangaretta,* bound for the South Pacific. A Methodist missionary and family were the only other passengers. After twenty-two days on the high seas, we arrived in the Philippine archipelago.

Our first home in Manila was on the campus of Bethel Bible Institute. A group from the Bible school, under the leadership of Floyd Horst, was waiting for us to arrive. For our church they had rented a hall for $115 a month. It was on the edge of the city limits about eight miles from downtown Manila. The area was called Tondo, the worst slum of the city. It was headquarters for harlots and gangsters. Many of the people of Manila were afraid to go into this section, especially at night.

The hall was an old vegetable market with steel bars on all four sides of the building. Alongside ran a foul-smelling open sewerage ditch. The stench was such that worshipers often sat through the services with a handkerchief held over their nose. Once I saw two dead pigs lying in front of the church, covered with flies.

Only forty people were present for my first service in the shabby old market that would seat three or four hundred.

Of those, twenty-five were students from the Bible School, and the others were visitors from other churches. I did not have one member that I could count on. This was quite an adjustment after leaving the great church in South Bend. Yet I was content, believing that my labor was by divine appointment.

Almost immediately after arriving in the Philippines I was invited up to Baguio. This city in northern Luzon was known as the gateway to the headhunter country. An American lady missionary, Elva Vanderbout Soriano, had asked us to come and preach to the primitive tribesmen among whom she labored.

Louise and I had been reading in the Manila newspapers warnings for vacationers to stay away from streams and waterfalls in northern Luzon's Mountain Province because headhunters were active in the area at that time. In the morgue at Clark Air Force Base I had seen the remains of two young servicemen who had wandered off into these forbidden mountains. All that was left of them were a few teeth-marked pieces, ankles and knees. They had been eaten completely by the cannibals. Perhaps their heads were hanging now in some remote native hut. As was my nature, I relished the challenge to carry the gospel to these lost souls.

Mrs. Soriano was a remarkable woman. When I first met her she had been in Baguio for thirteen years without a furlough. Her work was chiefly among the Igorots, one of the largest tribes of Luzon. It is noteworthy how she obtained the confidence of these primitive people, who do not normally trust outsiders.

A young Igorot boy was in jail in Baguio for theft. When the time came for his release the city officials did not know what to do with him. One day the chief of police met Elva on the street and asked if she would take the pagan boy and train him. She said "Yes," and thus, almost by accident, entered into a ministry to which she would devote the rest of her life.

Elva took the boy into her home, washed him, and gave him his first nice clothes. She nursed his lice and sore-infested body to health and taught him the ways of civilization and of Christ. He proved to be a very bright lad who learned quickly. He became a normal, happy youngster.

News eventually spread to the tribes people far back into the mountains that a white creature had taken one of their children. Some of the natives made their way through the dense tropical jungles to see how he was being treated. One day Mrs. Soriano noticed little black eyes peering out from behind the bushes at the edge of the jungle near her home. She was surrounded by headhunters.

They called the little boy over and asked, "What is the foreigner doing with you? Is she going to eat you?" She was the first white woman some of them had ever seen. Finding the boy well and happy they wanted to know why a woman from a foreign land would love their people. They invited her back with them to their tribe. This opened the door for her to tell these headhunting cannibals of the loving heavenly Father who cares for us all. Mrs. Soriano soon found herself caring for more and more of the destitute headhunter children. She earned a reputation as the "Mountain Mother of Luzon."

One of the peculiar beliefs of the Igorots was that whenever twins were born to them they thought one was the child of the devil. Their reasoning was that a normal woman could have only one child, so the other must belong to the devil.

Since they were not sure which one it was, they would usually kill both of them, or feed them to the animals.

Mrs. Soriano had made a ministry of rescuing these twins and rearing them. She would send older native boys into the jungle looking for newborn twins. Whenever she found a pair she would either beg them from the parents or threaten to report the parents to the Philippine soldiers who would come against them. These primitive people did not seem to mind giving their children away, rather than feeding them to the animals. Two of these orphans were named Lester and Louise, after my wife and me.

As the tribes became acquainted with Mrs. Soriano they invited her to visit their villages and preach the gospel of love. Many were won to Christ and little groups of believers sprang up among the headhunters. Some of the young people she sent to Bible schools in different parts of the Philippines to be trained for gospel work.

The Igorots of Mountain Province have an intricate system for legal, domestic, and moral laws. They have ceremonies for marriage, birth, death, war, religious and special festive occasions.

One of their most significant ceremonies comes upon the death of one of their warriors. Whether he is slain by ambush or in direct battle, his body is immediately brought back to his own hut. Here his corpse is placed in a sitting position in a *sung-a-chil,* or death chair. The women and children of the family dance around the dead man shouting to him to take revenge upon his killer. While the ceremony is going on the widow remains in a nearby village and mourns the death of her husband alone.

Several days after the man's death, the warriors of his tribe dress for a war dance. They create a special headgear made of betel nut palm, and put red leaves around their wrists and legs. Then they dance slowly and intricately toward the dead man's house. They begin about one kilometer away, beating their cymbals with a human jawbone.

Upon arriving at the house of the deceased, the witch doctor performs a ritual involving a pig sacrifice, with prayers to the war deities to grant a successful revenge upon the killer. Then the warriors feast on the pig meat.

After the feast the body is placed on a stretcher and the dead man's arms are tied to two sticks bent crosswise over the corpse. Four men carry the body to a burial cave and place it in a sitting position with the head supported by a stick against the wall. Years later, the bones fall to the ground, but the skull will remain hanging on top of the stick.

After the burial, the warriors meet for another ritual ceremony. The priest cuts off the head of a live chicken in the midst of a circle of warriors. They watch as the headless fowl flops about. Wherever it stops, the man toward whom the bleeding neck points is selected to avenge the death of the slain warrior. With spear in hand, he begins a head hunt that will not end until his mission is accomplished. Thus one death leads to another. From generation to generation the feuds between warring tribes continue.

For unnumbered centuries some of the headhunter people have eaten human flesh. They believe that this demonstrates their power and superiority over the enemy. Warriors boast in the number of human skulls hanging around the walls of their huts as a display of their strength.

The headhunters are not the same race of people who live on the plains and inhabit the cities of the Philippines. Some anthropologists associate them with the Mongolians from the Chinese mainland. Others think they are related to the Malayan group, or even with the same strain as the American Indians. Whenever God divided the peoples of the earth, for His own purpose, these aborigines were isolated for centuries from other cultures and civilizations. They are a strange looking people, small in stature, and with primitive features. However, those who leave their culture to attend school often prove to be intelligent and creative. Some have become successful in the professions of the outside world.

About the time of Abraham, the Igorots began to dig their now world-famous rice terraces out of the granite mountainsides. These green-terraced mountains comprise some of the most fascinating and spectacular scenery I have ever seen.

Civilization had come slowly to these forgotten people who for millenniums have lived in the mountain fastness of Luzon. Only an occasional corrugated steel roof or battery-powered radio gave witness that this was the twentieth century. Even the armies of Imperial Japan could not subdue them. But God's time had come for the Igorots.

I felt no fear when our evangelistic party started into the high Cordilleras of Mountain Province, Luzon. I knew that God was with us. There were, as yet, no roads to many of Luzon's towns and villages. The area included some of the most rugged mountain terrain I have ever encountered. The dense jungle country was ripped by serpentine rivers and covered with fog that hugs the high mountain tops. To reach inland villages we had to walk for hours, crossing streams and rice paddies and rugged hills.

Our evangelistic party of over twenty people was almost like an army. We marched into the mountains carrying our food, stove, and beds with us. In a remote village we occupied a little house, hanging sheets to separate the men from the women. Those who did not have a cot slept on the floor.

Having a foreigner present attracted the entire tribe to our meetings which were held in the open air in front of a little building. Lanterns were hung around and the natives sat cross-legged on the ground.

During the course of my sermon one night, an Igorot lady began to make strange noises in an effort to disturb the meeting. I raised my hand, looked at her, and in a loud voice demanded, "You shut up and never speak again."

At the time I did not know she was the chief witch doctor of the village.

When my interpreter repeated my command the power of God seemed to descend and the woman went into a violent fit. I spoke to her again, "I said shut up and also be still."

The witch doctor was quiet. From that day on she was never able to contact the devil again. Satan's power over her was broken. God's victory became the talk of the tribe for many months to come.

It was my great joy to see several of the Igorots accept Jesus Christ as Savior. Upon conversion they immediately forsook their old ways. Through Christ they became a peaceable, friendly, and loving people.

Ministering deliverance to the headhunters was exciting and I enjoyed it immensely. In a way it was tempting to devote more time to these tribes. After all, that is what many people think missionary work is all about. These were the kind of experiences people loved to hear about in missionary conventions back in the States.

But my heart was in the bustling, throbbing city of Manila, and most of my efforts were concentrated there. The city is where the teeming masses of people were. I knew that hell could be just as hot for the urbanized, educated heathen of Manila as it would be for the headhunters. And I was responsible to bring to them the message of redemption through Jesus Christ.

Those first six months in Manila were extremely frustrating. At the end of that time I was still at point zero. I had thought I could do here what I had done in South Bend, but things just weren't working for me. I had several apparent converts, but when I went to follow them up I found that they had invariably given me the wrong address, and probably a fictitious name.

It was obvious we would never establish a strong indigenous church without a more desirable location. I began to look for a lot downtown on which to build a church even before I had a congregation. I was certain that God had sent me to build a great evangelistic center. It was to be the most important edifice in Manila, even more so than the government buildings, and I needed a proper location.

At the corner of Taft Avenue and United Nations Avenue, at one of the major intersections of the best part of town, was a site made vacant by bombs from the recent war. This lot was bordered by a government office building, a new Y.M.C.A., the Red Cross building, and the American Bible Society which was around the corner. By the kindness of Rev. Paul Pipkin and help from friends back home, the $20,000 necessary to purchase this choice piece of property was secured.

Just prior to our first Thanksgiving in Manila, I received a cablegram from Australia from evangelist A.C. Valdez, Jr. The message read, ''If you and your church will support my meetings I will come to Manila for a city-wide crusade and I will guarantee all the expenses.''

I immediately held a meeting of all the members of my

church (that was just my wife and I). We sent a cable back to Mr. Valdez saying, "The church is 100 percent behind you. Send me some money to advertise the crusade."

It was ridiculous to even think about holding a city-wide campaign in my impoverished, ratty building. After praying about the situation I went to see the manager of the San Lazaro race track. He had never heard of such a thing as religious services being held at a race track. "Isn't it kind of funny, having meetings out there where the horses race?" he asked.

"No, it's not funny," I answered. "You have this stadium here and that's what we need."

"Why don't you go to one of the churches?"

I optimistically told him, "The people we are going to have couldn't be accommodated in any church. We are going to have thousands of people here and they are going to be saved and healed."

His eyes brightened up. "You say people are going to be healed?"

"Yes, God will heal them."

"Listen," he said, "I have a brother who is a paralytic. If you will guarantee me he will be healed you can have the stadium rent free."

Without hesitation I put my faith to the test, "Okay, I'll guarantee that."

He then told me that I would have to pay for the fifty janitors that cleaned the place up. The cost was about $300 per day. I agreed to pay the bill for two weeks.

Immediately I had some handbills printed to publicize the meeting. Floyd Horst, another missionary, and I went around town at midnight putting the announcements on every vacant wall we could find. We placed an ad in the large *Manila Times* that went to all the islands of the country.

For the opening service of the crusade we had about twelve hundred people present. They almost filled one box section of the immense stadium. The second night our crowd was a little larger and each night the number grew. Scores even came by boat from the various islands of the archipelago. Before the crusade was over a nightly attendance of about five thousand people filled the entire box section of the stadium. We never did get out to the bleachers.

Over twenty thousand stood for salvation during the two weeks, but many of these were the same people standing again each night. Ten thousand came through the prayer lines. After every service we prayed for the sick and suffering until past midnight. I noticed that the same people were coming through the prayer line again and again.

I felt that in spite of the apparently great meeting, we were getting nowhere. I wasn't sure these people understood what salvation was all about. I thought after the meeting was over and the evangelist gone, I might be back in my ramshackle church with nobody. The Lord impressed me to announce that those who wanted to be baptized in water should meet at Manila Bay on Sunday afternoon. Hundreds raised their hands that they wanted to be baptized as Jesus had been in the River Jordan.

To my amazement, thousands were at the waterfront that Sunday afternoon. I talked plainly to the crowd, discouraging as many as I could. I wanted to make sure that those being baptized were making a genuine commitment. ''You must live a clean life and pay the price if you are baptized. You may be in trouble because of this. You must be sure that you want to do it.''

That afternoon, 359 men and women were baptized

by immersion in the name of the Father, and of the Son, and of the Holy Ghost. Our church was born that day in the warm water of Manila bay. Those who were baptized stayed with us. I was thrilled to see how they sanctified their lives and began to show the fruits of holiness. The Spirit did this work within them without my having to harp on it. Also I noticed that the standard of living of these people began to rise as they followed the Lord and He prospered them. Among these were many who later became pastors and evangelists.

Before our first year in Manila had lapsed, we had 423 in our Sunday school. Congestion in the old building was terrible. We even had a whole class for naked children. About fifteen or twenty kids came who had no clothing, so we put them in a class by themselves to keep from mixing them with the other youngsters.

After purchasing the lot in downtown Manila, I found a B-52 hangar owned by the Pepsi-Cola Company that was not being used. The hangar must have been worth at least $50,000 but the Pepsi people sold it to the church for $10,000. Charles Blair in Denver helped me raise the money for the hangar by contacting several of our friends in the States. We received no denominational support for this large building. We simply trusted God day by day to provide.

We found a builder to put up the hangar and an architect to design a lovely front and interior with a balcony. The hangar made a surprisingly beautiful building with a Cathedral-like dome rising over forty feet into the air. Forty-foot steel and glass windows adorned each side of the structure. To me it was the most impressive church edifice in the country. A large sign over the church declared, ''Bethel Temple, Christ Is The Answer.'' Our church became known as the ''Christ Is The Answer Church.''

But before we completed and moved into our new facility, I would experience one of the most astonishing cases of divine deliverance in modern times. That miracle was to become the key to a spiritual revival that would shake the entire nation. Manila and the Philippines would never be the same again.

9

Seventeen-year-old Clarita Villanueva had suddenly become the most talked about person in the Philippines. Her name captured top headlines in the Manila press, and even the world press picked up and carried the story. Every hour on the hour radio newscasts gave updates of the sensational story of this young provincial girl who had been picked up on the streets of Manila for vagrancy, and placed in Bilibid Prison.

On May 13, 1953, *The Manila Chronicle* carried this report under the headline, "Police Medics Probe Case Of Girl Bitten By Devils:"

"Police medical investigators last night failed to give a convincing explanation to the puzzling case of the girl who claimed she was being attacked by demons, and who substantiated the claim with marks on her skin.

"At least twenty-five competent persons, including Manila's chief of police, Col. Cesar Lucero, say that it is a very realistic example of a horrified woman being bitten to insanity by 'invisible persons.' She displayed several bite marks all over her body, inflicted by nobody as far as the twenty-five witnesses could see. Villanueva writhed in pain, shouted and screamed in anguish whenever the 'invisible demons' attacked her.

"Fr. Benito Vargas (Roman Catholic), chaplin of the NGH, who witnessed Villanueva in her fits, said it was not his to conclude any verdict. But he said the fact remains that 'I saw her bitten three times.'

"Villanueva claimed she had been seeing the 'invisible persons' since last Sunday. She claimed the Phantoms were two—one tall, evil-looking, dark, and garbed in black, and the other short and cherubic, with snow white hair. She said the latter did most of the biting.

"Villanueva was perfectly normal between fits.

"After talking for a while, she would shout, have convulsions and hysterics, all the time screaming, and her eyes flashing with fire. Then she would point to a part of her body being attacked, then fall almost senseless into the hands of investigators. Teeth marks, wet with saliva, mark the spots she pointed at.

"All the time, all witnesses aver, she was never able to bite herself."

I did not read these exciting reports of the young girl bitten by devils until after she was delivered. The thing that forced me into the story was a special forty-five minute radio broadcast over station DZFM. I had never heard such a bloodcurdling program in my life. Immediately following the ten o'clock evening news, the radio announcer began the program by dramatically stating, "Good evening ladies and gentlemen. If you have a weak heart, please turn your radio off!"

I had a strong heart. Reaching for the radio dial I turned the volume up.

Instantly a series of piercing screams blared through the radio speaker, followed by pandemonium. The voices of several doctors could be heard through the confusion—"This can all be explained;" "Our records show that this phenomenon has been known before;" "This is epilepsy;" "It is extreme hysteria."

Other persons were excitedly saying: "The girl is being choked by some unseen thing. She is blue in the face and there are marks on her neck." Another would say, "Look, the marks of teeth appear!" Then Clarita would scream again. Such a haunting, tormenting scream it was—the scream of a girl possessed. I had dealt with those who were demon-possessed before. There was no doubt in my mind that Clarita Villanueva was in desperate need of divine deliverance.

I was not able to sleep at all that night. Over and over the cry of the possessed girl rang through my ears: "Help me, help me. They are killing me!"

I went into the front room of our home and walked the floor. I laid on the floor crying, "Oh, God, you can cast the devil out. Please deliver that poor girl in the city jail."

After I prayed thus until 6:00 A.M., God definitely impressed my heart. "If you will go to the jail and pray for her, I will deliver her."

At first I strongly resisted the idea of going to pray for Clarita. After all, doctors, scientists, professors, legal experts, and even spiritualists had tried to help her, and all had failed. Here I was trying to build a new church in the center of Manila, and I just could not afford the adverse publicity that might come from getting involved in this case. And then, who did I think I was anyway to suppose that in a city of several million, I, an unknown American, could get an interview with such a notorious person as the mayor. However, I learned that where God's finger points—there His hand will make a way.

The next morning I was granted an interview with Mayor Lacson of Manila. The mayor was visibly shaken by the hopelessness of the doctors before such strange phenomena. He stressed that he could not promise me any safety, for the girl was violent. However, he agreed to allow me to pray for Clarita, if I could get the approval of Dr. Mariano Lara, chief medical adviser of the Manila Police Department.

At Bilibid Prison I met Dr. Lara, a professor and department head of Pathology and Legal Medicine at the Manila Central University, and professorial lecturer of Legal Medicine, University of Santo Tomas. Sitting on a bench in the long, drab prison morgue, I heard this respected physician say that in his thirty-eight years of medical practice, he had performed over eight thousand autopsies and that he had never found a devil yet. He told me that he did not accept the theory that there is a nonmaterial force existing in the universe. But this baffling Filipino girl, being bitten by unseen assailants, had changed his philosophy of life. He turned to me and whispered, "Reverend, I am humble enough to admit that I am a frightened man."

Dr. Lara had reason to be afraid. Psychoanalysis, potent drugs, and even truth serum had all been tried, but "The Thing" persisted in attacking Clarita. A medical doctor who accused her of doing this for a publicity stunt, died within four days after she shook a finger at him and said, "You will surely die."

Until I spoke with Dr. Lara, he had thought religion offered no answer for Clarita's dilemma. The Roman Catholic chaplain of Bilibid Prison, the archbishop of Manila, and the priests of the Roman Catholic healing center at Baclaran had all refused to pray for her. A group of spiritists had conducted a seance in Bilibid Prison. Afterward, they declared it was the spirit of John the Baptist biting the girl. The medics refused to go along with this deduction and asked the spiritists to leave. I realized that my first hurdle was to convince Dr. Lara that I knew what I was doing and that I could help the girl.

I reasoned with Dr. Lara that there are only three powers in the universe. First there is the "positive power," or the power of a creative and benevolent God. There is also the "human power," or the power of men like ourselves here in the earth. Then there is the malevolent and sinister "negative power" of the devil. I asked Dr. Lara, "Do you think Clarita is acting under God's power?"

Thoughtfully, he shook his head. "No, it couldn't be God's power."

"Then, do you feel that, with your experience in treating humans, she is acting like any human being?"

He hesitantly admitted that this encounter was with something that was beyond doubt "supernatural."

"Then," I assured him, "there is only one power left. She must be acting under demon power."

Continuing my line of reasoning with Dr. Lara I said, "If there is a negative force in the universe over which a positive force has no control, our universe would go to pieces. If there is an evil which no right can correct, then evil is mightier than right. This cannot be. If this girl has demon power in her, then Jesus Christ can deliver her from that power."

Opening my Bible, I read from the Gospel of Mark 16:17, "And these signs shall follow them that believe; In my name shall they cast out devils. . ." Dr. Lara was amazed to see that Christ had commissioned His church to exorcise evil spirits. He did not know that casting out of devils was in the Bible.

I volunteered my services to pray for the girl and cast the evil spirits out of her. The doctor assured me that I would be welcome. I then requested that no medication be given Clarita until the next morning, explaining that if Jesus healed her He must have all the glory. We made an appointment for me to see Clarita at 8:30 the following morning.

After fasting and spending much of the afternoon and evening alone in prayer, I went to the jail the following morning. Entering the prison grounds, I saw a swarm of doctors, police officers, photographers, and newspapermen, representing the local and foreign press. My immediate thought was, "Boy, now you've done it. You have really made a fool of yourself." But I prayed silently and rejected that thought as the voice of Satan.

Dr. Lara led me down a dusty prison road through barbed wire gates, to a dreary little chapel. We were followed by a motley crowd that had not the slightest idea what they were going to see. About one hundred spectators, including many women prisoners, crowded the small chapel. I was the only Protestant among them. I was gratified to find that these onlookers were friendly and even sympathetic. Most of them had already witnessed the failure of the doctors, the psychiatrists, and the spiritists. I sensed that they had hope, if not faith, in God's power to answer my prayer. But they were of no spiritual assistance to me.

After we all were gathered in the chapel, Dr. Lara ordered that Clarita be brought in. As the frightened girl entered the door she observed each person slowly and closely. When she came to me at the end of the line, her eyes widened and she snarled at me and hissed, "I don't like you." I recognized that it was Satan speaking through her lips. The voice had been in English, yet Clarita spoke the Tagalog dialect. She could not speak English and after she was delivered I had to converse with her through an interpreter.

I had Clarita sit on a wooden bench and drew up a chair in front of her. "Clarita," I began saying, "I have come to deliver you from the power of these devils in the name of Jesus Christ, the Son of God."

Suddenly the girl went into a fit of rage. "No! No! They will kill me!" she screamed. Her body became rigid and she lost consciousness. I grabbed hold of her head firmly with both hands and cried, "Come out of her you evil and wicked spirit of hell. Come out of her in Jesus' name!"

She immediately regained consciousness and began to rage again. The doctors said that this was the first time she had instantly come back from one of the trances that so baffled them. With hot tears streaking her flushed face she begged me to leave her alone. She pointed to her neck and stuck out her arm to show me the fresh wet marks where she had been bitten at the moment. I was shocked. There were human-like imprints of teeth so severe that some of the small blood vessels underneath the skin were broken.

A holy anointing came upon me and I entered into the greatest spiritual battle of my life. I was angry at Satan and I rebuked him in the name of Jesus. Satan in turn blasphemed through Clarita's lips and cursed the blood of Jesus in the vilest language.

After a long and violent struggle the girl seemed relieved. The demons refused to speak again or to bite her. Some of those present thought the demons were exorcised but I told them that the battle was not yet over. It was nearly noon and I was soaked with perspiration and exhausted.

I told Dr. Lara that I would go home and fast and pray another day and return the following morning. My faith was

tested that afternoon when one evening newspaper published my picture on the front page, three columns wide, with
the headline, " 'The Thing' Defies Pastor.'' Another
newspaper gave a more optimistic headline: "Devil Loses
Round One.''

Upon arrival at Bilibid the next morning, the captain of the
prison said that Clarita had not been bitten since the prayer.
But the fact that she was not completely delivered yet was
evident as soon as the devils saw me. Clarita again became
Satan's mouthpiece as they cried through her, "Go away!
Go away!''

Faith welled up within me and I spoke back with a thrilling feeling of authority, "No, I am not going away! You
are going away. This girl will be delivered today!''

I requested every person present to kneel and help me
pray. I warned them against mocking or laughing for when
the devils came out of Clarita, they would surely seek another
victim. Doctors, newspapermen, police officers, and professors knelt humbly as I prayed. However, a woman
prisoner nearby was making light of the affair and when
Clarita was delivered, this inmate was bitten and immediately
lost consciousness. The newspapers carried her story that
afternoon.

The extra day of fasting and prayer had made a difference.
As I commanded the demons to come out they seemed to
realize it was their last struggle. They cursed and cuddled
their victim for a few violent moments and suddenly I felt
release. Clarita relaxed. The glazed other-worldly look left
her eyes. She smiled.

An indescribable peace enveloped us. The atmosphere in
that little Catholic chapel was electric. Around me I saw
newspaper reporters weeping. Doctors were wiping their

eyes and otherwise hard-boiled jailers were visibly moved. I began to sing softly and others joined in singing with me:

Oh, the blood of Jesus
Oh, the blood of Jesus
Oh, the blood of Jesus
That washes white as snow!

I asked Clarita if the demons were gone and she answered weakly, "Yes."

"Where did they go?"

She turned her head and pointed toward the steel-barred window.

We were ready to depart when the girl suddenly screamed again, sending a terrifying chill of horror over everyone present. The demons had returned!

I cried to them, "Why have you returned? You know you must go and not come back."

Speaking in English through her lips, they replied, "But she is unclean and we have a right to her."

The demons had no power to resist. They departed and she became normal again.

Through an interpreter I explained to Clarita what had happened and got her to pray with me for forgiveness of her sins. She invited Jesus Christ into her life and received Him as Savior and Lord. Then I taught her to pray and plead the blood of Jesus against the devil.

From my experience I knew that the demons would no doubt make one more attempt to victimize Clarita after I was gone. I instructed her that when this happened she must demand them to leave "in Jesus' name."

As I predicted, that same evening at eight o'clock, Clarita let out a bloodcurdling scream. She shouted to the guard, "Help, they are back to get me! They are standing behind you!"

The horrified guard jumped up on his desk and in shock watched what he calls the greatest struggle he had ever witnessed. He could not see the aggressors, but he could see the hysterical girl in mortal combat. In desperation she cried to the guard, "Oh, what did the American Father (minister) tell me to do? Tell me quickly!"

The guard, still on the table, shouted back, "Plead the blood of Jesus. He said to plead the blood of Jesus."

Clarita screamed, "I plead the blood of Jesus. Go in Jesus' name."

At that instant she lurched forward and grabbed with her hands which seemed to have been suddenly freed. She went into a coma. By this time prison authorities and many prisoners had appeared. They laid Clarita onto a table, and noticed that her fists were tightly shut. A doctor pried her hands open. To his utter astonishment there was a clump of long, coarse black hair in her palm and under her fingernails. Dr. Lara placed this hair into an envelope and put it in a locked vault. Under a microscope it was later determined that the hair was definitely not human. It could not be identified as belonging to any known creature. This phenomenon I must leave unanswered for the present.

The moment Clarita was delivered, Dr. Lara asked me to go with him to the office of the mayor. Walking past a flock of secretaries we were ushered into the inner office. Once before the mayor, Dr. Lara triumphantly declared, "Clarita has just been delivered. The devils are gone!"

Mayor Lacson stepped out from behind his desk and grabbed my hands to thank me for my help. "If there is anything we can do for you," he offered, "just let us know. We will be happy to do it." Later the mayor's kind assistance would prove invaluable to our ministry in Manila.

The next day I left the province to get away from publicity. My only motive in praying for Clarita had been a sincere desire to see a tormented girl delivered from the power of the devil. However, my picture appeared on the front pages of newspapers and in magazine articles throughout the Philippines and in some other parts of the world. My ministry and work became known all over the archipelago. This unsought publicity gave me an influence for good that otherwise I might never have achieved. This was the miracle that opened the hearts of the people of Manila to the full gospel, and prepared the way for the great revival which followed.

Another thing that helped prepare the hearts of the people of Manila for revival was Oral Roberts' film on divine healing, *Venture Into Faith.* I had prayed that God might supply a print for the Philippines, but I had made no solicitation or contact with Oral. However, as I was praying in Manila, God was also working on the other side of the world in Tulsa, Oklahoma. Brother Roberts not only sent me a print of the film, but also a projector and a large screen. I showed the film to the pastors belonging to the Philippine Federation of Christian Churches and in turn was invited to show it in many places in Manila and throughout the islands. With Ruben Candelaria, superintendent of the Manila District of the Methodist Conference, we set up a series of three night crusades in which we would show the film, preach deliverance, and pray for the sick. Aside from the churches in Manila, we conducted crusades in the provinces of Bulacan, Rizal, Nueva Ecija, Pampanga, Bataan, and Mountain Province. No auditorium was large enough to accommodate the crowds that flocked to those salvation and divine healing campaigns.

The mass distribution of deliverance literature was also

a contributing factor to revival. Shortly after my arrival in Manila, Gordon Lindsay of Dallas, Texas, felt led of God to send me thousands of back issues of his magazine, *The Voice of Healing.* Each month when I received the large bundles I had them put in my office. I felt that God wanted me to use these magazines but I wasn't sure just what to do with them. I had only a small congregation and limited means of distribution. The stacks kept growing higher until they literally reached from the floor to the ceiling of my office.

Now with the large crowds coming to our campaigns throughout the Philippines, I seized the opportunity to inundate the nation with this deliverance literature. In a way impossible to calculate, the printed page helped prepare the hearts of the people of the Philippines for revival. The thousands who read these magazines were made hungry to see the miracle power of God demonstrated in their own city.

I was glad for the opportunity to minister the gospel in the crusades we were holding, and I thanked God for the hundreds who were being ushered into the kingdom of God. At the same time, it was thrilling to watch the progress of the local church I was building. Crowds had grown so that our old building could not begin to accommodate them. On January 25, 1954, we occupied the impressive new Bethel Temple in downtown Manila. The building was debt free the day we moved in. Attendance soared and in the first few weeks that building was also overflowing with as many as twenty-four hundred in Sunday school.

Yet, my heart was restless. We were barely scratching the surface of the great masses that needed to be reached with the gospel. I wanted to do something really meaningful for God.

I remembered that the mayor had asked if there was anything he could do for me. There was—and I went to ask him.

I made an appointment to see Mayor Lacson, who was now a good personal friend, and requested use of the famous Roxas Park for revival meetings. This park is literally the very heart of the nation. Strategically situated in front of city hall, one block from the congress buildings on the south, and one block from the great post office building on the north, it is the best known location in the Philippines. The mayor was true to his promise. In less than one minute he granted me the use of the park for one month. For two years God had been preparing the way for this revival. This was zero hour.

With the mayor's permission, we converted the famous Sunken Gardens of Roxas Park into a great outdoor cathedral. A speaker's platform was erected, lights were installed, and the park was staked out and roped off in sections to accommodate the anticipated crowds. God sent us an expert team of volunteers from Bethel Bible Institute, the Methodist church, and professional people in the media, who were a tremendous help in promoting the meetings.

Thousands of handbills were distributed. Daily news releases were published. Class-A air time was purchased and paid for by Rev. David Candelaria and the Methodist church of Taytay, for a daily broadcast on the most popular radio station in the nation. But our best advertising was the thousand or more people who had already been saved and healed that went with us to the city park meetings. Some of these people had the most amazing testimonies of divine healing I had ever heard. Several of them gave their testimonies publicly on the first night. News spread like wildfire that miracles were happening in the Sunken Gardens, where a huge sign proclaimed: *Christ Is The Answer.*

The Lord sent us Rev. Clifton Erickson to minister to these masses of people. They came from all over the Philippines, representing every stratum of society. They came by airplane, by boat, by bus, by truck, by jeep, by horse-drawn cart, and on foot.

By noon each day the people would begin to congregate in Roxas Park. By three o'clock, about a thousand people would be occupying the best seats in front of the platform. By six, several thousand were waiting for the service to begin. And when service got into full swing at eight o'clock, the park was a sea of faces, upward to thirty thousand and often more.

Although the more sensational ministry of deliverance no doubt helped draw the crowds to the meetings, the salvation of souls was our top priority. My consuming passion was to rescue souls from hell. Strong appeals were made to the sinner nightly. The response was simply overwhelming.

In the afternoon services at the church, Rev. Robert McAlister ministered and there were always from two hundred to six hundred who made decisions to follow Christ. In the great open-air services each night there were from five thousand to ten thousand who responded to the appeal. Some nights toward the end of the revival, there were thousands more. I am almost afraid to estimate how many made decisions during the thirty days, but the total was a staggering figure—possibly between one hundred fifty thousand and three hundred thousand souls.

One night a thunderstorm interrupted the service, but hardly a person moved. The rain could not chase them away.

Many had come prepared and the sea of faces became a sea of brightly colored umbrellas. Despite the weather it was a glorious service with hundreds claiming their healing and thousands making decisions for Christ.

Perhaps the most thrilling revival scene I have ever witnessed was on Sunday night, February 14th. At the conclusion of my sermon that night I asked for "men only" to give their hearts to Christ. Thousands of men raised their hands.

I then spoke plainly to these men, explaining what it would mean to become a real Christian. I talked about the life of holiness and instructed them that this meant they must stop drinking, going to movies, gambling at the cock fights, etc. I told the men they would be expected to change their life style and cultivate the habits of prayer, Bible reading, and church attendance.

"Now," I said, "if you desire this kind of life, come to the front for a prayer of salvation."

They came! Five thousand strong they came! To my joyful amazement men crowded around the platform in the large open space where the sick were normally prayed for. It was, I believe, one of the greatest moments of my ministry. I could see tears streaming down the faces of scores of men standing in front of me. If they had looked up, they could have seen that tears were running down my face, too. I felt like I was about to be raptured. It was the first time such a scene had ever been witnessed in the history of the Philippine nation.

As a result of that revival, Bethel Temple soon became the largest Protestant church in the Orient. The enthusiasm of our people would be hard to imagine. For instance, one Sunday I announced that I would like to see who could bring the most to Sunday school the next week. One man brought three hundred. He rented three big trucks, rounded the people up, and hauled them in. Soon we had ten thousand people registered in our Sunday school with a weekly attendance of seven thousand to eight thousand. To make room for all the people, we had Sunday school on Saturday afternoon and four services on Sunday. Church began at 7:00 A.M. and continued until late Sunday evening. The great B-52 hangar was packed to overflowing every service.

We added full-time pastors to our staff to minister to those who spoke various languages. Services were held in Ilocano and in Tagalog, each with their own pastor. I preached to the English congregation and also the Chinese with the aid of an interpreter.

The results of that great revival extended beyond the capital city of Manila. Soon Bethel Temple became a "mother" church for a second church in Quezon City, a third in Niac, a fourth in Pasig, and a fifth in Caloocan. Branch Sunday schools, outstations, and preaching centers followed. Hardly a village or city in the area did not feel the impact of the great revival in Manila and the "Christ is the Answer" church.

When Oral Roberts was invited to Manila for a crusade in Roxas Park we took him to meet the president. As Oral started to pray, President Magsaysay looked at Brother Roberts and said, "In this country we have learned that Christ *is* the answer."

Crowds as high as twenty-five thousand attended the Oral Roberts crusade. It was at first frustrating to Oral not to be able to lay his hands personally on every individual of the great masses who came nightly for prayer. But on the final Sunday afternoon of the campaign, Oral decided he must at least *try* to touch each one who desired prayer. He had the people form a double line that extended for three city blocks. It took him four hours to walk between the lines, laying his hands upon each one as he ministered to them. Oh, how the people were blessed!

The end of this great move of God was nowhere in sight. I expected to remain in Manila for a very long time. But God had other plans.

We in the western world have a difficult time comprehending the oriental mind. The common people of the Philippines considered me almost as a God. In the church they were extremely devoted to my spiritual leadership over them. Many times people would fall on their knees on the street and kiss my hands before I could stop them. If I were standing in a line, as at the post office, people would recognize me and fall out of line to allow me to move ahead of them.

Possibly for this reason God began to deal with my heart about leaving the Philippines at the height of revival there. I knew that if I stayed the people would be inclined to worship me instead of God. I did not want to leave, but God spoke to me that another must now lead these souls whom God had given me.

This was a very difficult thing for me to accept and I prayed, "Lord, there must be further reason for you to want me to leave."

There was another reason. Within the next two weeks I received a cable from America. It was sent by the pastor who had followed me to South Bend. The cable read, "I am leaving as of next Sunday. The people will have no pastor. Do what you wish about it." As I read the cable, tears came to my eyes. I knew what God wanted me to do.

10

Immediately after reading the cable that said the congregation in South Bend would be left pastorless, I booked a flight to the United States. While my family remained behind in Manila, I was at Calvary Temple in South Bend the following Sunday morning. I had cabled the people that I was coming.

The minister who had followed me was already gone. Although I found the people somewhat discouraged, I have never been more warmly received anywhere than I was that morning. It was a highly emotional time with much rejoicing in the Lord. Without voting, the church received me back as their pastor by unanimous acclamation.

I soon learned that during the two-and-one-half years I had been in Manila, the South Bend congregation had sunk deeply into debt. Attendance at the church had not gone down appreciably, but they were about thirty thousand dollars in arrears in current accounts. Things just hadn't been managed very well. Their credit rating with utility companies, supply houses, etc., had been ruined.

That Sunday I began a two-week revival meeting at the church. God blessed mightily and the place was packed with people each evening. We raised several thousand dollars during those two weeks, enough that the financial situation at the church reversed itself. I stayed in South Bend for a total of six weeks getting things in order and then flew back to Manila, preparing the church for my permanent departure.

When we first moved to the Philippines we had been a family of four. Now we were five. Our youngest son, Peter, was born in Manila on October 17, 1953. The Filipino people seemed to have a special love for Peter because he was also "their" baby.

Moving back to America from the Philippines was very difficult. When people have such an honest and primitive admiration for you, as the Filipinos did for our family, it is a frightening thing. The display we witnessed at the Manila airport the day we left was enough to convince me that I did the right thing in leaving the great church there to the ministry and leadership of another pastor.

Thousands were in the airport to see us off. As we boarded the plane people began to cry in an almost hysterical way, and some fainted.

The captain of our international flight was so upset by the scene that after the plane had taxied out to the runway, he turned it around and came back into the airport. The captain came back to me and said, "Sir, I think you had better go back out to those people. I can't take this plane off with all of them out there screaming for you. I don't know who you are, but those people want you."

Louise and I disembarked. We walked up and down the fence that separated the people from the runway, trying to console them. "We will be back every year," we promised, "and we will always be close to you in our spirits. You have other fine pastors to watch over you now and you are going to be all right."

Publicly and privately we had tried to teach the people that their great love was to be for the Lord Jesus. We admonished them that their security was completely in Jesus Christ and that they were to follow Him rather than any human being. But these people, coming newly to Christ, had a difficult time understanding.

When we moved to Manila we had gone with many tons of equipment, such as an organ, an icebox, kitchenware, and appliances. When we returned to the United States we carried only a suitcase. And that was within the forty-pound limit allowed for international air travel. We left to the incoming pastor our automobile, our home, our furniture, and even the pictures on the wall. We had freely received these things as the blessing of God, and now we freely gave them to another.

Back in South Bend it almost seemed a dream that we had ever been away. The crowds surged, the work expanded, and the blessing of God was phenomenal. Calvary Temple grew even larger than it was before we left, and continued to be the largest church of any description in the entire South Bend area. The day school, the day nursery, the book store, and all our ministries continued to move forward.

During this time we, with other ministers, invited Oral Roberts for a crusade to be conducted in the Northside Gymnasium in Elkhart. This crusade was a great boost to us as well as all the churches of the area.

We remained as pastor of the church in South Bend for several years. At the same time the congregation understood my calling and burden for world evangelism. They gave me freedom in traveling to minister in various parts of the world.

One spot I particularly enjoyed visiting was the new nation of Israel. So enthralled did I become with the prophecies being fulfilled in the Holy Land that I developed an insatiable desire to understand fully the things that God was doing there. Also, the Lord showed me from the eleventh chapter of Romans that I was to be a blessing to the people of Israel.

In August of 1956, I took a six months' leave of absence from my pastorate. Robert McAlister, who ministered with me in Manila at the Roxas Park crusade, came to fill in for me while I was gone. During these months I lived with my family in the city of Jerusalem.

My wife was not too happy about going to Israel at first. She was frightened by the prophecies of war that would befall that nation in the last days. Half-teasing she said that she could just see me being one of the two witnesses slain in the streets of Jerusalem as foretold in the Book of Revelation! However, when I assured her that God was the one leading me to Israel, she was ready and willing to go.

It was not just a vacation or a sightseeing tour. We went to Jerusalem to accomplish a task for God. While there I served as the regular preacher in one of the churches. A Jewish man was the pastor, but he didn't like to preach, so he asked me. On Sunday evenings I held ''Prophecy Rallys'' in the Jerusalem Y.M.C.A. building. At other times we went all over the territory talking to small groups and ministering.

As in the past, Louise proved to be a real asset to me in Israel. She quickly fell in love with the people, who also developed a special love for her. She was especially effective in dealing with the Israelis she met on a person-to-person basis.

For example, we bought our meat at a kosher shop. The butcher would save the choice cuts for Louise. When she was in the shop, he would wait until the rabbi was out of earshot and whisper, "How much bacon do you want today, Mrs. Sumrall?" He kept the pork hidden under the counter for her.

But it wasn't always easy to witness to the Jew. When Louise tried to speak to her hairdresser about the love of God, he just glared at her. Pulling up his sleeve he revealed the ugly marks that had been inflicted on him in a Nazi concentration camp and snarled, "God is love? I saw my own sisters thrown alive into the furnace. And then they tell us we are God's chosen people. Humph!"

To souls such as this it was not a matter of telling them about the *love* of God. It was a matter of trying to convince them that there was a God at all.

One night I had a home meeting in Tel Aviv, with about fifty Jewish people present. My theme for a talk that night was "altars." Taking my Bible I began with Abel's altar, going right straight through to Calvary's altar. I stressed the blood—and especially the blood of Jesus.

When I had finished, one of the men present, a rabbi, spoke up. "Those are interesting fairy tales," he said, "but why did you waste your time and ours by telling us that?"

He had come expecting a lecture on psychology, or the working of the mind. He wasn't upset because I had talked about Jesus. His trouble was that he didn't even believe in the God of the Old Testament.

This rabbi went on to say, "I used to laugh at my fathers for believing our forefathers who wrote that tale about swimming across the Red Sea, and here you are talking out of the same book as if you believe it. I tell my children that those things are fairy tales. Our fathers didn't have anything better to do than to sit around the fire and gossip. They made up those stories."

I looked at the rabbi in amazement and tried to reason with him. ''Can't you see that God brought the Jewish people from all over the world to make Israel a nation again, in fulfillment of prophecy?''

''God didn't have anything to do with it,'' he answered. ''Nobody wanted us.''

We quickly learned that the real problem in evangelizing the Jew was not to get him to accept Jesus, but to get him to believe in God.

After we had been in Israel for only a short time, we went to Tiberias on the Sea of Galilee for a preaching mission. The night after the service, we slept on the bottom floor of a little place that was just below ground level. All night long we heard the rumble of heavy trucks speeding down the road just over us. I turned to my wife in the bed and said, ''Honey, that's not normal. Something unusual is happening.''

We remembered that earlier in the afternoon we had noticed many of the young men of the city grabbing their coats and running out of their homes and shops as if they were in a terrible hurry to get somewhere. We feared that they might be rushing off to war.

Everyone in the area had been expecting hostilities. The threat of war had predominated the radio news for several weeks. We could pick up broadcasts from Egypt, Saudi Arabia, Jordan, and other Arab countries, as well as Israel. None of the newscasts sounded good.

The next morning it seemed to us that all the men of the city had evaporated. We went downtown to the bank and did not see a single man there—only women.

I began to inquire, ''Where are all the men?'' In a whisper a teller behind the bank counter answered, ''They've gone to war.''

I turned to my wife and said, "Honey, let's go home."

As we drove back to Jerusalem we saw what seemed to be thousands of tanks. All of them were covered with camouflage. All of them were on their way to meet the Egyptians. Israel had entered what became known as the Sinai War. We lived through this nightmarish time of blackouts and terror.

After I got Louise and the boys back to our apartment, I set out to see the war. To me it was exciting to know that I was actually experiencing firsthand some of the fulfillment of latter-day prophecy. Looking back I sometimes wonder why I was not more afraid.

I applied for and received permission from the government to travel through the battle zone. A military escort armed with machine guns rode in my car with me all the way down to the Suez Canal. When we ran low of gas (there were no service stations open) we would just stop a tank and siphon a few gallons of petrol to get us on down the road.

We saw the instruments of war captured from the Egyptians. Dead bodies were scattered along the road and live bombs lay sprinkled over the desert.

I walked over to Mt. Zion to an Israeli machine gun nest with six or eight machine guns in a circle dug into the side of the hill. I just walked right in, sat down with the soldiers, and struck up a conversation. I picked up one of the machine guns, examined it, and asked, "How do you shoot one of these things?"

One of the soldiers readily demonstrated for me how the gun worked. After a while another soldier asked, "Are you an officer?"

"Well," I hesitated, "I don't think so."

"Then who the blazes are you?"

"I am an American press correspondent."

The soldier advised, "You had better get out of here, buddy. You just might get yourself killed."

In fact, I was a correspondent. During this time I wrote numerous magazine and newspaper articles about the Israeli-Egyptian conflict in the light of Bible prophecy. I also published my own prophecy newsletter which was circulated around the world.

When the war began, the American consul strongly advised us to leave Israel immediately. They even offered to provide free transportation for all Americans to evacuate, and were very upset when we refused to go.

On one day our three boys went to the British school they attended with over three hundred classmates. The following day the Sumrall boys were the only students present. Everyone else, including some of the teachers, had evacuated the country. Even the American ambassador was gone. Insofar as we knew, we were the only family of Americans left in Jerusalem.

To me it was no great decision to stay. God had sent me to Israel for these months and I could not see leaving the people just because they were having a war. Anyway, it made no difference to me if I went to heaven from Israel or from the United States.

The Israelis seemed to be impressed and appreciative of the fact that we did not run off and leave them. We became endeared to the hearts of these sad and embattled people. It was not unusual for one to grab and hug us when we met them on the street.

By the end of March the war had ended, and so had our six-months leave of absence. The time had come to resume our pastorate. We were reluctant to say "good-bye" to Israel, but anxious to get back to South Bend.

11

For the next two years God continued to bless our ministry in South Bend, but I could never reconcile myself to the fact that my work for God was to be confined to this local congregation. God began to deal with my heart again about the plan He had given me some years earlier for evangelizing entire nations by building a strong indigenous church in the capital city.

The place that particularly bore on my heart was not exactly the capital of a nation in the normal sense. It was more of a city-state, the burgeoning British Crown Colony of Hong Kong—threshold to China.

China had always been very near to my heart. As a teenage evangelist, shortly after the Lord had given me that vision of the nations of the world, I dreamed of being somewhere in China. In the dream someone came to me in the night and said, ''Come with me and pray for a woman.'' I went to a humble little Chinese hovel and prayed for a woman who was instantly healed. It was a simple dream, but it had remained strong in my mind and had haunted me for all these years.

The year that Howard Carter and I had spent in China on the first trip around the world had in many ways been the most thrilling year of my life. Now the doors to missionary work in mainland China were closed. I had the feeling that if a strong church were established in Hong Kong, it could become the launching point for a great missionary movement into China once the doors swung open again. It would not only be a lighthouse to the four million inhabitants of Hong Kong but the church would serve as a recruiting station to train Chinese youth who would be prepared to gather the harvest on the mainland when the time was ripe.

A.C. Valdez, the evangelist who held the first city-wide crusade for me in Manila, had recently been through Hong Kong. He had come to me saying he felt impressed to encourage me to go to this hub of the Orient and raise up a work for God.

While pastoring in South Bend I had gone to Hong Kong with Gordon Lindsay for crusades and I saw the tremendous potential there. The heart of that great city was virtually untouched with the full gospel message. Many of the higher class Chinese people of Hong Kong spoke English, having been educated in the British schools. Thousands of these business and professional people were neither Buddhist nor Christian. They were adherents to no religion at all. I saw this as a golden opportunity for a gospel outreach.

After much fasting and prayer I definitely felt that God was directing me to this island metropolis to establish a church. My wife's heart, as mine, had always been in missions. She was anxious to share this new venture of faith with me.

In 1959 I resigned my pastorate in South Bend for the second time. I did not feel that it was fair to impose upon these good people by continuing to leave and come back to them. I have never had any relationship with that particular congregation since that time. They have continued to be a strong growing church and a powerful lighthouse of the full gospel.

Before moving with my family to Hong Kong, I made several visits to the city. There I contacted some key Chinese men and formed a committee to help in an evangelistic thrust in the colony. They were anxious to see a work established which would reach the total populace of the city. We were also joined by half a dozen men from the Hong Kong chapter of Full Gospel Business Men's Fellowship International. They were excited about winning souls for the Lord Jesus.

On one of those visits to Hong Kong I took a team of other ministers with me, including John Meares, Thomas Reid, Morris Cerullo, and Gordon Lindsay. We rented a football stadium and held a successful crusade. Up to five thousand people attended the meetings each night. At the conclusion of that effort we baptized the people who had given their hearts to the Lord. There were sixty-nine of them. These became the charter members of our church.

Land is almost impossible to buy in Hong Kong. In Manila, a World War II bomb had cleared the site for our church. But in crowded Hong Kong there was simply no property available. If a lot could have been found large enough to put a church on, it would have cost a million dollars or more.

We bought the entire fourth floor of a tall office building. That floor alone cost us 250,000 Hong Kong dollars (about $50,000 in American money). It was a new building located downtown by the post office and right on the waterfront. In the same building, the Communist party occupied the seventh floor, the Roman Catholics had the third floor, and many other organizations and businesses, such as Minolta Cameras and the Chung Khiaw Bank, shared the remainder of the building. We converted our floor into an auditorium that would seat about three hundred people and named it "New Life Temple."

By the time Louise and the boys moved with me the church was already organized with a good nucleus of people. Our home was a lovely little apartment on the side of Victoria Peak on Hong Kong island.

Our congregation in Hong Kong was made up mostly of people who fled out of the southern part of China when the Communists took over their land. Over half the people in Hong Kong were refugees. People were constantly trying to come into Hong Kong from the Chinese mainland. Barbed wire fences were erected to keep them out and police patrolled the beaches. Yet, scores of refugees continued to pour in, many of them swimming from the Kwangtung coast of southern China.

It was a very sad place to minister because of the poverty, families separated from ones left behind on the mainland, and the high incidence of suicide. We had a church of people who knew what sorrow was. They knew what it meant to be persecuted, abused, and deprived. They held their freedom dearly.

We enjoyed several victorious revival crusades in Hong Kong and God performed many miracles in our midst. One was with Rev. Clifton Erickson—an outstanding healing of a lady who had come into our church out of Buddhism. She had a huge ugly goiter which hung down like a grapefruit in front of her neck. For years she had been unable to button the collar of her Chinese-style dress because of this deforming growth. When she was prayed for this lady didn't notice that anything special happened. But the next night she returned and testified of being healed. The goiter had dried up and only a loose bag of skin remained. That too tightened up in a few weeks.

As a result of her conversion and healing, this lady won her entire family to Jesus Christ. Her son was a brilliant young man who later felt the call of God on his life to enter the ministry. He saved his money and came to the United States to attend Gordon Seminary in Boston.

The attitude of the Chinese Christians toward denominationalism was refreshing. For example, it was not unusual to find those who attended Episcopalian services on Sunday morning and a Pentecostal church on Sunday night. They, no doubt, had been baptized in both churches—just to be sure they were right.

If you asked them why they attended two different churches, their candid answer was: "In the morning I go to the Episcopalian church to get peace, because they are so quiet. In the evening I go to the Pentecostal church to get joy so my heart will be glad."

These Chinese saw nothing strange about attending "high" and "low" churches. They refuse to have the same ill feelings between denominations as do many Christians in America. There was also a closer unity among the clergy of different Christian denominations. Perhaps it was because they needed one another more.

In many instances, the various denominations actually reach different strata of society. Usually when a church began with poor people, it would still be made up of the same a generation later. But if a church began with a stable, middle-class people, it is doubtful that it would ever reach the poorer classes. The poverty stricken generally prefer the fellowship of those on their own level. How beautiful it was to see denominations actually supplementing the ministry of one another, rather than engaging in battle against each other.

God helped us at New Life Temple to do that which was unusual for Hong Kong. Our church was able to reach all classes of people—but not all at once. You just can't go in and break down deeply ingrained cultural traditions. And that wasn't our task. Our goal was to win men to Christ, even if we had to reach different classes of people by holding different services for them at different times. It worked out that we had three totally distinct congregations who worshiped at New Life Temple. It was never planned that way. There was no way we *could* have planned it. But God miraculously helped us to simultaneously reach all classes of people, instead of being confined to one group as are most churches in Hong Kong.

Those who attended on Sunday mornings were no doubt the wealthiest group of people I ever served as pastor. Among our members were many very prosperous and highly educated business and professional people, factory owners, doctors, etc. The services for these people were mostly in English. At other times I used an interpreter and the meetings were bilingual.

On Sunday night the peasant class came to our services. These included destitute refugees, servant people, etc.

On Friday night we had a congregation made up largely of small business people such as shopkeepers and fishermen. These included the "boat people"—those who lived in their Chinese junks that were moored in the harbor.

One of the affluent men who came to our Sunday morning services owned a large factory where he manufactured batteries for the Eveready company. He lived with his wife and five beautiful daughters in one of the most gorgeous homes in Hong Kong. This elite family came to church faithfully every Sunday morning, but to none of our other services.

After they had been attending our church for some time I suggested to the man, "We would also like to see you bring your family to services on Sunday night."

The man replied, "You mean I need to come Sunday night again. You mean I have to get all these girls dressed up and pay the fare across on the ferry twice in one day." As sincere as he could be, he asked, "Where in the Bible does it tell you to go to church twice on Sunday? If you've got more to tell us, then keep us an extra hour on Sunday morning."

Once or twice he visited our Sunday night services, but I didn't make an issue of insisting that he come. I realized that my responsibility was not to instill American customs into the Chinese people. I was only to share Jesus Christ with them. And if that meant having different services, at different times, for different classes of people, then I was the one who needed to adjust and not them.

Our water baptismal services were particularly beautiful in Hong Kong. We tried having one baptismal service at a swimming pool at one of the clubs in town. But my favorite site for many baptisms was one of the famous beaches reached by ferry from Hong Kong. A long flight of stairs led from the road where our buses parked down to the beach.

One of our converts, Brother Aw-Young, was a business-man who had been healed of a stroke. This man exported shark fins all over the world and had offices in Hong Kong and in San Francisco. Although healed, he had not regained all of his strength. So determined was Brother Aw-Young to be baptized that he had his servant take him out to the beach every day for three weeks to practice going up and down those stairs. It was beautiful as the congregation rejoiced with him on his baptismal day.

The young man who kept our church in Hong Kong was named Aming. He had slipped across the border as a refugee and had no relatives in the city. For weeks Aming slept in doorways and lived on the streets of Hong Kong, until one day he was invited into the church by one of our ladies. He became our janitor and was so happy to live there in New Life Temple. We learned to love him so much. I gave him his first shoes and his first coat.

Aming developed a real interest in spiritual things and his life was completely transformed by the gospel. He went to school at night and qualified for a job in a bank. Today he is a certified public accountant, a respected citizen of Hong Kong, and still a faithful follower of Jesus Christ.

New Life Temple never approximated Bethel Temple in Manila, but it became a very strong evangelistic center, which it remains to this day. New Life Temple also became the mother church to a second congregation in the British Crown Colony.

We had an extensive literature ministry in Hong Kong, printing over one million books, tracts, and pamphlets in the Chinese language each year. These were not only distributed in Hong Kong, they were sent to every place where there were Chinese-speaking people—Singapore, Indonesia, the Philippines, Taiwan, and Malaysia.

Hong Kong was only an hour and a half from Manila, by air. This gave me the opportunity to keep in close contact with the work there. I traveled back and forth often, establishing new churches in the Philippines. The buildings were built on the same pattern as Bethel Temple. The mother church was built out of a B-52 hangar, the others from military Quonset huts. They made a very beautiful tropical building, especially when an architect designed the front. They would seat three hundred to four hundred people.

We also found time in our rigorous schedule to conduct several revival meetings throughout the Orient. We went to Malaysia, Java, Singapore, and Bangkok, Thailand for these crusades.

After spending more than two years in Hong Kong, the church was firmly established in truth and in Christ. I felt it would be a waste of time for me to just stay there and supervise things. God had called me to do pioneer work. I found a fine minister, Rev. William Thornton, who felt the call to the Chinese people and to Hong Kong, and left New Life Temple in his care. The church property had been in the name of the congregation from the beginning. As in Manila, we gave the new minister our car, our apartment, our furniture, and the things that had taken us over two years to accumulate.

I was now forty-six years old, but it seemed I had already lived six lifetimes. For all of these years I had been a pilgrim, never holding the things of this life too dear. My suitcase was packed. I was ready to follow wherever God's Spirit would lead me next.

12

From Hong Kong my family moved back to South Bend, Indiana, and established headquarters. We organized and incorporated the Lester Sumrall Evangelistic Association (LeSEA) which became the base for worldwide missionary work. Our outreaches included crusade evangelism, radio, the publishing of *World Harvest* magazine, and many other avenues of ministry. Our consuming purpose was the establishing of evangelistic centers in strategic capital cities of the world from which to penetrate the entire nation.

One of the cities in which we sought to do this was Brasilia, the progressive, futuristic new capital of Brazil. Clearly it is the most modern capital of the twentieth century.

They call it the ''City of Hope''—a glistening jewel seven hundred miles into the interior of Brazil's vast territory. Planted like an island of modernity in the heart of the world's largest unbroken jungle, it rises like a science fiction dream city from the scantily explored territory inhabited by Indians as primitive as Stone Age men.

Brasilia is a perfect example of the strange contrasts that marks the world's fifth largest nation, the eighth most populous country on earth. My heart was particularly drawn to this Latin American giant. Brazil is a country of fabulous wealth, bursting with promise not yet fulfilled. Experts say Brazil is the only South American country capable of becoming a great world power, yet multitudes of its people live in poverty to the point of starvation.

Brazil has been steeped in a religious tradition for generations, with 95 percent of the people calling themselves Catholic. Yet, nearly half of her eighty million people are bound to some degree by the satanic bondage of spiritism, a devilish system brought over by African slaves and mixed up with Indian animism.

I was still in Hong Kong when I first began to feel a strange leading to go to Brazil's fabulous new capital. At the same time, unknown to me, God was dealing with the heart of a veteran missionary, Virgil Smith, in Santos, Brazil. He too felt led to Brasilia.

Virgil Smith had first gone to this South American nation in 1927 as a representative of the Church of Christ. But he was hungry to have the same power as the men of the first New Testament church, and he sought God for a deeper experience. Then, months after he began his Brazilian ministry, he went out into the woods to pray and received a glorious infilling of the Holy Spirit. This began a career in pioneer missions, raising up churches and establishing congregations, and helping build permanent places of worship for these new Christians.

God brought Virgil Smith and I together in Brasilia. With some other men of God, we began to see miracles take place as we secured lots downtown on which to build.

I never did actually move with my family to Brasilia, as I had to Jerusalem, Manila, and Hong Kong. Instead, we maintained our home and headquarters in South Bend, Indiana, and made several trips to Brazil for two to six weeks at a time.

On one of those first trips to Brasilia, we conducted a successful tent and open-air crusade. We were delighted to find the city ripe for evangelism. Many of the people who attended our crusade services had been involved in spiritism and Satanism. They were eager to hear a new gospel—a message of power and deliverance. This was demonstrated forcefully when every night up to 95 percent of the sinners present in the audience responded to the appeal to accept Christ as their Savior.

I went to see government officials about securing select property in the new capital for a church. It was to be the first Full Gospel church in the city. I was successful in obtaining three acres of choice land—a full city block—in an ideal location. The services of a brilliant Brazilian architect were secured to draw plans for the new center, and construction was begun.

Our first building was a school, with a large auditorium. While this building was being erected, we moved the revival tent to the property where it served as our church sanctuary for fifteen months. About the time the school auditorium in our evangelistic center was being completed, a fierce storm struck Brasilia. Hurricane force winds ripped the big canvas cathedral to pieces, leveling it to the ground. Fortunately, we were soon able to move into the school auditorium.

Another outstanding missionary, Norman Anderson, helped with the building and establishment of the new church and school. Then, a few years later, Virgil Smith was able to leave his own center of ministry in the state of Sao Paulo, and came to work with our Brasilia center.

A second evangelistic center was established in one of the suburban centers near Brasilia, in the satellite city of Taguatinga. Here a new church was built which would seat approximately four hundred.

While we were busily involved in establishing the new work in Brasilia, as well as crusade and literature evangelism and missionary endeavors in other parts of the world, the devil reared his ugly head in Manila. The move of God there had so shaken his kingdom that it was inevitable he would strike back with everything in his power. Satan seemed determined to neutralize and to destroy the testimony built up by the revival fires which had swept the Philippines.

Knowing that attack and persecution from the outside would only strengthen the church, the devil employed the the strategy he has found so effective through the centuries—trouble and division within the church.

In 1962, satanically inspired confusion and chaos developed in the Manila congregation. In all my experience in many countries, I had never witnessed anything as heartbreaking as this, especially since I was the father of the work. The foundation of the nationwide testimony was threatened by Christians quarreling and fighting among themselves, instead of presenting a united witness to the world. This agitated my soul beyond description.

The battle began among the very ones who should have prevented it—the ministers. It came to a hopeless deadlock and division between the missionaries and the congregation. Things became so bad that the resident missionary was asked to leave the pulpit and return to America.

Other missionaries took sides in the dispute. One even posted a large sign on the front of the church forbidding people to worship in a house of prayer that had been dedicated to God. For a period of two months, guards were posted at the entrance to the church. Their very presence served to discourage people from attending. As unchristian as it may seem, there were several cases pending in court on both sides.

I felt impelled of God to return to Manila to see if I could find some means of bringing peace out of a seemingly impossible situation. I loved and had very close association with both factions. I realized that both sides were sincere in believing that they were right, and yet both were being used of Satan to destroy the work of God.

I negotiated with all parties concerned for several days without success. I met with them the last time and told them—all of them—that if they had been the father of the work as I was, and if they loved the work as I did, there would be no fighting.

Later two of the brethren met and decided the only solution to which both sides would agree would be for me to accept again the spiritual leadership of Bethel Temple. It was not at all my intention to resume the pastorate of the church in Manila. I was fully occupied with many projects around the world. However, in order to save one of the greatest revivals of this generation, I agreed to return. The missionaries unanimously accepted me on the field; the members of Bethel Temple voted unanimously for me to return. After praying diligently, together with my wife and three sons, I felt impressed of God to take up the challenge again where I had left off some years before.

God marvelously helped us to bind up the wounds at Bethel Temple. Within weeks, old animosities began to disappear. Ill feelings and misunderstandings were forgotten as God rebaptized the church in a spirit of revival.

I recognized Manila as a formidable bastion of spiritual strength from which to evangelize all of Asia. The Philippines is the only Christian nation in the Orient. I foresaw that if increasing hatred of the white man continued, it was likely that Filipino Christians would become the missionaries of the future.

The Orient is a place of one billion souls, and Manila is strategically located in the center of this vast population. In an hour-and-a-half one could be in Japan, Korea, or Indonesia. In the approximately eighteen months we stayed in Manila this time, I used it as a base from which we bombarded the Far East with tons of full-gospel literature, as well as preaching the gospel in crusades and by radio.

I had all intentions of remaining in Manila and using that city as the headquarters for my ministry, when God dramatically showed me that I had accomplished my task and the time had come once again to depart.

I received a letter from President Marcos of the Philippines inviting me to sit in congress as his guest for the state of the union address. On one side of me in the congress hall sat the archbishop of the Roman Catholic church and on the other sat the American ambassador. I enjoyed the ceremony and the address and was grateful for the opportunity to attend.

When the congress was dismissed and we departed the building, we were greeted by a mob of maybe twenty-five thousand angry demonstrators. They were chanting and waving signs saying, "Go Home White Monkeys!" "America Is Imperialistic!" etc.

I walked out among that crowd of Communist-inspired demonstrators and made my way back to my church which was only two blocks away. I was upset. As I entered my office, pondering in my mind the things I had seen and heard, I began to weep.

In the years I had ministered in the Philippines I had refused to let anyone think I was anything but a Filipino. I absorbed their thinking. I tried to look, dress, talk, and act like one of them. When Jesus, the Son of God, came to earth,

He referred to himself as the Son of man. Why? Because he came to identify himself with you and me. I had tried to follow this example of Jesus in every place I had lived.

When I was in Hong Kong, I was no longer a Filipino; I was Chinese. I once told my church in Hong Kong, "If you ever call me a foreigner, I'll leave the next morning. I'm more Chinese than you are. You're one by accident of birth, and I am one on purpose."

Yet I could not change the color of my skin or the slant of my eyes. I could not erase my heritage. I was an American. Even though my church in Manila loved me, Americans in general were becoming increasingly unpopular in the Philippines. It hurt to think that many lost souls who needed the gospel would not even give me a hearing because of their hatred for my homeland.

God spoke to me at that moment. "America is in worse shape than even this country. You should go home and minister to those people permanently."

That evening I broke the news to my wife, telling her what the Lord had told me. In a few weeks we found Rev. Dan Morocco and family to replace us as pastors of the church. We made our last move back to the United States.

Our nation *was* in worse condition than the Philippines. Surely the mid-1960s was one of the darker hours in our national history. Unrestrained madness was erupting with a fury on university campuses across the land. Violence was rampant at political rallies and conventions—as in Chicago. The drug culture was rapidly becoming a fact of life in every town and hamlet, no longer confined to the big cities alone. Almost overnight the sexual revolution had become a scourge that was destroying the land. The "beatnik" of the fifties had evolved into the "hippie" of the sixties. It was a new generation of young Americans whose life style was wrought with sin, sickness, and filth.

It was with a sense of divine destiny that we returned to our home in South Bend. We knew that we would continue to travel around the world in pursuit of souls, but for the rest of our lives our base of operations would be America, my own native land.

I wrote these words which seemed to sum up my feelings upon our return. They appeared on the front cover of the September 1965 issue of *World Harvest* magazine:

The Cry of a Native Son

America, I love you.
I am a son of your native soil.
I am most at home in your big cities.
I have drunk deeply of your freedoms.
I have enjoyed your abundance.
But, America, can you not see the ''hand-writing on the wall?''
Your enemies are deadly within and without.
You have poisonous vipers posing as your friends.
They are ready for a fatal thrust.
America, you bear the hatred of many lands.
I have heard you cursed in foreign tongues.
I have seen you misunderstood by men and nations.
You are unloved and unwanted in a world of peril and need.
America, worst of all you are sick inside.
I see your newsstands filled with pornographic reading.
I see your clothes styled by sex deviates.

I see your lust for pleasure like a Roman delight.
America, I see you worshiping the golden calf of material greed.
You need Christ. . .**NOW**.
You need His love, His delivering power.
America, it may not be too late for you to find God now.
God save America—land that I love.

13

It was 10:30 on a Saturday morning in South Bend, Indiana, that God spoke to me. "In Jerusalem I will show you what I want you to do for me."

This was startling! Jerusalem was at least six thousand miles away. I almost wanted to ask, "Why Jerusalem?" But without asking, I remembered that throughout history God had often spoken to men in Jerusalem—the Holy City.

A short time later I was in Jerusalem on one of the many visits I have made to Israel. Awakening early one day, I walked briskly from my hotel room in the crisp morning air. I made my way to a craggy rock overhanging the valley of Hinnom, near the barbed wire border that did divide Israel from Jordan. It would be sunrise in fifteen minutes. Already the skies were lighting up with magnificent hues of red and purple and gold over the hills of Moab.

I looked tenderly to my left toward Zion's Hill and the ancient walls of old Jerusalem. Directly before me, at the peak of Zion's Hill, was the Upper Room, where the Last Supper was held, and to which the apostles had returned seven weeks later to be endued with the power of the Holy Spirit at Pentecost. I could see the road to Bethlehem, and the Jaffa Gate which was no longer in use—before the war of 1967.

To my right was the famed Wailing Wall. In the distance rose the beautiful Mount of Olives and the Garden of Gethsemane where our Master wept over Jerusalem, and from whence he ascended to heaven, leaving a promise to return.

I had been here on numerous occasions before. This was my most treasured place to pray. Often from this spot I had watched the sun rise over Jerusalem. I had stood many times, transfixed as columns of light marched through the narrow streets of the ancient Holy City.

I was in deep prayer and meditation. Just as the brilliant sun was beginning to crest over the horizon, bringing light and heat for the day, God spoke to my soul:

"You are responsible to take one million souls to heaven." The Lord made it clear to me that He did not mean a million hands raised or a million decisions, but a million souls landed safely in the arms of Jesus.

Staggered at the awesome task, I asked, "Lord, it is impossible. How can this be?"

Before me I could see a lone man plowing a furrow with one small camel. The furrow was neither wide nor deep.

The Lord said, "When a man plows alone, like the Arab farmer with a wooden plow behind a camel, he does not accomplish much. He digs only a few inches deep into the soil and moves so slowly that in the evening he can see where he started in the morning. But, if you plow like the Israeli farmer, with a tractor piercing deeply into the soil and many furrows wide, you can bring a million souls to heaven."

God showed me that plowing deep is my personal relationship with Him. Plowing wide is my working with others of the same spirit. I must recruit others to help me in the harvest. Only with strong hands clasped together can this victory be won.

The Lord showed me many things that morning. He revealed to me how I was to utilize the mass media as never before, placing the gospel message on film and in print. Since I could be in only one place at one time, these tools would be the means by which I could multiply my ministry. God's truth of divine deliverance would be sent out to places where I could never go.

I was so thrilled with this new word from the Lord, I hardly knew where to begin. My being was almost transfixed as the hot Mediterranean sun rose high above the hills of Moab in all its life-giving splendor. As I walked the few blocks back to my hotel room, I felt a power that only the great Creator could have put within me. Suddenly I knew God's time had come to set more people free than ever before. It was God's hour to defeat the forces of hell. My course was set before me and I must run as I had never run before.

As I returned home to South Bend after hearing so forcefully from God in Jerusalem, my mind was a whirl. There was so much that God had laid upon my heart to do. I must produce deliverance films that would portray the power of God over the devil. I must increase the publication and circulation of full gospel literature. I must proclaim the gospel by means of radio and television. I must establish a school for the training of young ministers to go into the harvest field. I must continue and increase missionary and child care support around the world. I must accept the ultimate challenge of pioneering Christian television as the ultimate great alternative to the sadistic sex-exploited amusement of modern TV.

Back in America, I soon discovered that I needed a group

to pray with me and for me. I needed a strong home base from which to operate in order to be effective. Without that I was limited in many ways. I received a kind offer from Denver, Colorado. One man tried to give me a building if I would move my magazine and missionary headquarters there. I had other offers from cities from California to New York, saying please come and build a work here. But after praying about these I somehow could never feel the assurance that God wanted me to accept them.

One day a petition was handed to me with sixty-nine signatures on it requesting that I start a church of divine deliverance and power in South Bend. This group was without a church home and was meeting in the basement of the home of Ernest Eastburn. They had invited me to lead their Bible study on several occasions before when I had been in town. I did not know what to do. It had been a number of years since I had pastored in South Bend. The world had gone through many changes.

To be truthful, my attitude toward South Bend was somewhat like Nathanael's attitude had been toward the sleepy mountain village of Nazareth. He asked, "Can there any good thing come out of Nazareth?"

South Bend, Indiana, has its similarities with Nazareth. It is a midwestern town, between the Great Lakes, with Lake Michigan on its west and Lake Ontario on its east. The Peninsula of Michigan is above it, and the plains and farmlands of Indiana below it.

In our generation, South Bend has not been a rapidly growing or developing city. People in other areas get the name mixed up with North Bend, East Bend, or just plain Bend. Those from great metropolitan areas often make curt remarks about it. One of my friends called the city, "A spur off

Chicago." Not many people would think anything of much value could spring from South Bend. Yet I knew that the very breath of two national spiritual movements came from this city.

It was in the city of South Bend that a group of Spirit-filled Swedish Baptists were having a prayer meeting in a home in about 1910 or 1911. The Lord spoke to this little group and said, "Go to Para."

These saints of God did not know where Para was so they looked in an atlas and found that it was a state in northern Brazil. Two of those praying were Mr. Gunnar Vingren and Mr. Daniel Berg. They said, "We feel led to go to Para."

This faithful group of believers did not even have a church building of their own. Yet, the same night an offering was taken for these men to travel to Brazil as missionaries. They began their full gospel crusade in the city of Belem, Para. Since then the revival has spread throughout the nation of Brazil under various names. Formerly it was led mostly by Swedish missionaries, today mostly by Brazilians. It is by far the largest Protestant movement in the nation. Many of their churches in the cities of Brazil number four thousand to five thousand members. It is remarkable to me that this great thrust of God had its origin in South Bend, Indiana.

The second national spiritual movement I told of in an earlier chapter. That revival began the afternoon God spoke to me in South Bend and said, "Will you go to Manila for me?" I responded to that call and until this moment there is a move of God in the Philippines as has never been there before.

The remarkable thing is, it began in a place where many would say ". . . can any good thing come out of South Bend?"

Although I am very conscious of these things, I still was not sure I wanted to establish another church there. I delayed for some months before answering the call.

One of the ladies who had signed the petition, Virginia Kaelber, came to me one day and said, "Brother Sumrall, God spoke to me last night and said if you did not obey Him and open a church in this city that He would send someone else to do it, and that you would be jealous of the great work he would do."

As I had known this Christian woman for many years, I took her counsel very seriously. But still I could not come to a point of decision.

Later I was conducting missionary rallies in the state of Illinois. Early one morning in my motel room in Waukegan, I was having a time of communion with the Lord. God was dealing with me concerning building a church and international offices for our world ministries in South Bend.

I protested, "But my former church is there."

God replied, "They shall both be great unto me."

Then I remonstrated, "But the world is my parish and not a city."

The Lord very tenderly said, "Read Jeremiah 33:9." I opened the Bible quickly to see what message God had for me:

"And it shall be to me a name of joy, a praise and an honour before all the nations of the earth, which shall hear all the good that I do unto them: and they shall fear and tremble for all the goodness and for all the prosperity that I procure unto it."

I began to weep. This seemed too much. Surely God wanted me to establish the church and through it He would do a great work that would be a praise and an honor.

An hour later I wiped the tears from my eyes and went into the adjoining motel room where C.C. Ford and James Murphy were staying. As I read to them what God had said, the Spirit of God came upon them as a confirmation of His word. We all rejoiced in the Lord together.

I could see in this word from the Lord the ultimate fulfillment of the vision He had given to me as a young evangelist—the vision of reaching the entire world with the gospel. My ministry was not to be confined to South Bend. But from that base all the nations of the world would hear the gospel.

At the time that seemed an exaggeration to me. I did not see how it could be done. I could not clearly foresee the emergence of Christian television and satellite communications. But that was God's problem—not mine. He had made His will known to me. It was my duty to simply obey and leave the results to Him. We organized the church and named it Bethel Temple after the church in Manila, later changing the name to Christian Center Cathedral of Praise.

I do not believe I have ever done anything for God that has been more fervently fought by the devil, and by people, as was the building of this church. And possibly it was because of the very fact that God wanted it to be a praise and an honor before all the nations of the earth. The devil does not take things like that lying down. Yet it seems that every roadblock Satan placed in our path served only to give God another opportunity to demonstrate His miracle-working power. Whether it was the hand of God or coincidence is not for me to say, but six of the people who opposed us most vehemently came to an untimely death.

To begin our church we rented the facilities of the Progress Club, a ladies club downtown. The custodians of the club weren't very cooperative. They would not open the doors but would leave our people standing outside in all kinds of weather until 10:00 A.M. sharp, when our services were to begin. We were allowed to use the piano for our services, but our rent did not include use of the organ.

For many years my home had been located on a ten-acre piece of ground on East Ireland Road. When I first purchased this property it had been located out in the country. Over the years the city of South Bend had expanded southward until now East Ireland Road was one of the most heavily traveled thoroughfares of the city. This was a prime location for our church and my family and I willingly gave them the ten acres free of charge for that purpose.

Construction of the sanctuary and office complex began immediately. We bought three large metal buildings and put them together in a tasteful and beautiful triad. The addition of stone and glass made the edifice both beautiful and functional. The larger section was a prayer sanctuary. The left wing contained our offices and the right wing, educational facilities. The building had more than twenty-six thousand square feet on one level. We constructed the complex for $318,000, only a fraction of the million dollars it would cost to build a normal church of the same dimensions. To my knowledge this was the first metal church building to be erected in the United States. Since that time hundreds of others have gone up, many of them using our plans.

During construction I constantly reminded my growing staff that we were not just erecting a building—we were building a tool. I do not believe in building monuments to personal vanity or temples to human triumph. Our center is simply an instrument for world deliverance.

We officially dedicated the spacious and efficiently designed new facilities on Easter Sunday, 1967. An impressive and varied congregation from many cities in the Michiana area and many other states gathered for the event. Among our honored guests were my brothers, Ernest and Houston, and my brother-in-law, James Murphy. These three men have been Full Gospel ministers for many years.

When we began construction of the headquarters facilities, we did so by faith, with no funds. The way the money came in day by day was one long series of miracles. It came from South Bend and from all over the world. The New Life Temple Church in Hong Kong gave $10,000. Friends of mine gave sacrificially. All the miracles that God wrought for us in this undertaking I hope to share in a later volume.

God has been true to His promise. In the years since the construction and establishing of our headquarters in South Bend, our ministry has truly been ''a name of joy, a praise and an honour before all the nations of the earth.''

The souls that we had won for Christ in all our previous years of ministry had just been a warm-up for what lay ahead. God had been training me in His school of faith. Now I was ready to put that faith to the test. A million lost souls were waiting for me to respond to the challenge.

14

The multifaceted ministry that God has given to LeSEA (Lester Sumrall Evangelistic Association) is far beyond anything I could have ever dreamed. Our staff has grown in the last fifty years until we now have a team of over one hundred and fifty dedicated and highly skilled workers. When these words are printed our staff will have grown even more. Day by day the fulfillment of our vision is unfolding before us, and God is supplying laborers to help bring in God's final harvest. We are dragging in the nets with a million souls through the varied ministries God has given us:

Literature
The printed page was the first of the mass media. Until it was born, man communicated only by the spoken word. The world would not be evangelized today if it were not for the Bible. Many millions would not be saved if it were not for Christian books, tracts, etc.

While I was living in Hong Kong, bringing into being the New Life Temple Church, God spoke to me and said, ''The masses can be reached effectively through literature.'' I had just finished printing three million pieces of gospel literature in Chinese. I had seen my entire church congregation meet one day a week and go through the streets and large tenement houses of Hong Kong distributing this literature from door-to-door and person-to-person. We had felt its impact. We had seen its ministry.

An American pastor visiting Hong Kong at this time, between the airport and his hotel, was twice asked if he were a Christian and if he would accept gospel literature. This pastor, a personal friend of mine, was amazed that within his first hour in Hong Kong two people from our church witnessed to him about Jesus Christ.

The Lord said *World Harvest* would become my pulpit—that through the pages of this magazine I would speak to the world.

World Harvest magazine, our official bi-monthly journal, is sent to 107 nations. The messages of these magazines are constantly being translated into the different languages of the world and reprinted in other publications.

The greatest thing about *World Harvest* is that it is centered around the person of Jesus Christ. Every issue first and foremost exalts Him and His mighty deliverance offered to our generation.

When the world Olympics were held in Mexico City, I printed one million booklets in English, Spanish, and French. The message of this booklet was from the divinely inspired words of the Apostle Paul concerning striving for the goal and winning the crown. The message pointed to man's ultimate goal—eternal life through Jesus Christ.

Scores of churches in Mexico City cooperated with us by supplying workers to give these booklets out to the people. The impact of this effort was tremendous. We hired stenographers for several months after the Olympics just to answer the mail response of those who accepted Christ after reading the gospel message.

I have written more than one hundred books and booklets. Hundreds of thousands of these have been sold or given away and many of them have been translated into the various languages of Europe, Africa, India, Latin America, and other parts of the world. In South Bend our presses constantly print teaching manuals, tracts, and pamphlets.

World Harvest Films and Videotapes

It was that fateful morning on the rocky point, viewing the sunrise over the Judean landscape, when the Lord showed me that in the future there will be many millions of depressed and possessed humans who will need to know that God will and does deliver from satanic forces. The Lord directed me to produce documentary and dramatic gospel films featuring divine deliverance. We now have six such films in three languages, circulated in over fifty nations of the world. Nonpromotional in nature, these films demonstrate the power of God to set humanity free.

When my son, Frank, and his wife, Carol, were ministering in Indonesia, they visited a very large meeting and to their surprise one of my films was being shown. After the film was ended and an invitation was given, over five hundred people came to Christ that night.

We produce teaching series on many subjects. They are shown regularly on television and recorded on videotape for use in our Bible college and video schools around the country. God has given us excellent reproduction equipment for our mushrooming cassette ministry. The impact of these recorded messages is startling as hundreds write in to say how a certain tape has been such a blessing to them.

World Harvest Homes

I am personally a man of the big cities. I love great cities. I love masses of people. I was born in New Orleans, Louisiana. My heart throbs for New York, London, Paris, Rome, Chicago, Hong Kong, Manila, Singapore, and Calcutta. But in my office in South Bend, God spoke to my heart, "Give ye them to eat."

"Who, Lord?" I asked.

God answered, "You thrill to minister to crowds, but I have the homeless, the helpless, the orphans, all hidden behind closed doors who also need my love."

I did not want to get involved in the child-care ministry for any personal reasons. It began when my telephone rang at 3:00 one morning in South Bend. I answered the startling ring to hear the voice of Mrs. Elva Vanderbout Soriano calling transworld from the Philippines: "My children have no food; we have no money; we have no one to help us." Mrs. Soriano did not know that the Lord had already told me to help children and here was my first open door.

Immediately I replied, "A check will be on its way this morning as soon as I get to the office."

Thereupon we adopted over forty orphans in the highlands of Luzon. These are the children of the headhunters of the dense mountain vastness. I have never regretted entering this new venture.

From Baguio, we extended our child-care ministry into various tribes, then to Hong Kong, and later into Israel, Italy, and India.

Today we are helping support over three thousand children in fifteen nations. This ministry is expanding and will continue to expand under the anointing of the Holy Spirit.

Radio

Even before organizing the Christian Center Church in South Bend, we began petitioning the Federal Communications Commission for a construction permit for a new FM radio station. It was while we were building our new church that the permit came from the FCC.

By faith we began a $100,000 building program to put up a tower and studio facilities for WHME—World Harvest Missionary Evangelism.

The end of our long wait for the decision of the FCC was just the beginning of a four-year battle with the devil. He did not want our station on the air, and used every tactic to delay it and jeopardize its success. Although we owned about six acres of wooded property, the neighbors protested the erection of a tower in the area. Local officials balked at issuing a permit. Court hearings ensued and new complications developed. New land had to be purchased and FCC permits had to be extended and modified. One by one the pieces finally began to fall into place and God gave the victory.

Since 1969 WHME FM-103 has been reaching out to a sixty-five mile radius, twenty-four hours a day, blessing untold multitudes of people with totally Christian programing.

For a number of years, every weekday morning at 9:00 I personally presented a half hour open line program called ''May I Help You, Please.'' The hundreds of miracles of deliverance God wrought through this program alone could fill many volumes.

Television

At the time we started our Christian radio station, it seemed like a gigantic step. Little did I know that it was just a small training ground for a much broader and more effective ministry God had in store.

Soon after the radio station was on the air, God impressed me that Christian radio alone would not reach this generation. Television dominates America's free time. It has the power to control the minds of the masses and especially the youth. It can actually determine the destiny of a soul—or of an entire nation. Television is the medium of communication that will reach the world for Jesus.

We had seen the effectiveness of television while building our first church in South Bend. For several years we presented a prime time Saturday night program which drew hundreds to our church and reached many more for Jesus Christ.

However, the station took our prime time slot from us, banishing our program to an early Sunday morning hour when the people who needed the broadcast most were not watching.

Later, in building the Christian Center church, we had a program on one of the local South Bend stations. Because we were testifying of supernatural miracles of healing and deliverance on this program, the station manager gave us a mandate—"Modify your message, suppress the miracles, or go off the air." We would not compromise. We went off the air.

I was not alone in this experience. Such giants in Christian telecasting as Billy Graham, Rex Humbard, Oral Roberts, and Pat Robertson found it difficult to get prime time in major television markets across the nation.

One of the largest Christian broadcasters in the world told me he could see the handwriting on the wall. He predicted that there were very few years left in which any commercial time at all would be available for Christian television programs—at any price.

I saw the crying need of building a network of Christian television stations. When we began there were only five or six such stations in the world. Today there are several dozen. Any group can be licensed for a maximum of twelve stations. All of the Christian television stations in the world are owned and operated by evangelical gospel leaders.

Although I had had some experience, I did not understand the whole of television when I moved into it. Perhaps this was best, for had I known the complexity of this medium I might not have had the faith to tackle it.

I was offered the opportunity to buy a bankrupt million-watt television station licensed for the Indianapolis, Indiana area. This station, with its many cablevision outlets, has a potential of reaching between two and three million viewers. By faith I accepted the challenge of raising the $900,000 necessary to purchase this station. God honored our faith by performing miracle after miracle until we purchased Channel 40 and put it back on the air. We renamed the station WHMB (World Harvest Missionary Broadcasting) and introduced a format of family gospel programing. When we began broadcasting on November 3, 1972, we had a viewing audience so small that the station was not even listed in the ARB ratings for Indianapolis. The blessing of God, however, was upon this effort, and before long our ratings soared. Souls were saved and denominations began to flow together in friendliness and harmony.

The station had very little equipment when we purchased it and began broadcasting. We refused to purchase anything on credit, saying God would supply our needs and today we are the best equipped television facility in the state of Indiana, with several million dollars worth of the best electronic gear available.

From this station we began our cablevision ministry. This arm has reached out until our programs are now on over one hundred television outlets. Through other satellite networks we reach virtually every state in the country.

We acquired Channel 46 in South Bend, Indiana, a two and a half million watt station which had been in bankruptcy for two years. We renamed this station WHME (World Harvest Missionary Evangelism) the same as our radio station.

I feel that I am under direct orders from heaven to reach at least ten million people every day with the gospel message via television. Five days a week, my son, Stephen, and I co-host a sixty-minute call-in interview show, "LeSEA Alive." We feature special guests and a bank of manned telephones for handling incoming calls. Audience response has been overwhelming with an average of three thousand letters and three thousand telephone calls received each month. Also I have videotaped hundreds of hours of Bible-teaching programs.

We are taking our television programs produced here in Indiana and broadcasting them in Tokyo, the largest city in the world. They are also aired in Manila, and in the West Indies. Every day we are seeking new possibilities for reaching more people for Jesus Christ.

When I returned from Manila to labor for God in America, God promised me that on American television I would pray one short prayer and that ten thousand souls would be set free from oppressive demonic power!

In order to reach our goal we must have more stations—

new stations are being added as the Lord provides funds—and through them we will be able to reach the millions of people who must know the truth of the Lord Jesus Christ.

We have established an Earth Station with our facility in South Bend. This enables us to broadcast by satellite, reducing cost and increasing quality, reliability, and flexibility of our television transmission services. We have the capability of beaming out Christian television programing across the United States and around the world.

World Harvest Bible College

I was preaching in Brasilia, the new capital city of the great nation of Brazil in South America. We were having a good revival meeting and I was enjoying the blessings of God. For more than two weeks I had fasted without eating a meal, and at the same time was preaching twice a day. I had lost very little weight and felt strong physically.

During this time of seeking God's face I made what may sound like a selfish request of God. I prayed, "Lord, you have told others their position in life. You have shown others their life ministry. Would you be so kind as to reveal to me my future work?"

I remembered how the Lord had spoken to Peter that when he was old he would be led where he didn't want to go, speaking of the death that he would die. This prophecy meant Peter could not die young. Herod put him in jail in Jerusalem but could not kill him. Christ had prophesied that he would live to be an old man, and he was not an old man at that time.

I asked God to reveal to me my end and the ministry I must fulfill. As I prayed it seemed like a storm entered my hotel room. The power of God came upon me; I felt an unusual anointing of the Holy Spirit. The voice of the Lord spoke to my heart saying "It is written in Psalm 71:18."

I did not at the moment have any idea what was in that verse. I did not know what God was going to say to me. Kneeling beside the bed I opened my Bible and read: "Now also when I am old and grayheaded, O God, forsake me not; until I have shewed thy strength unto this generation, and thy power to every one that is to come."

I read that verse again and laughed out loud, "One thing is for sure—I am going to get old and grayheaded."

God was promising me that for the rest of my life my ministry would remain. My years would not reduce the strength and vitality of my work for God.

Then the significance of this verse came into focus. God said, ". . .Until I have shewed thy strength unto this generation." Not only was I to witness to God's strength but also to show His strength. I was to continue to pray for the sick and see them healed. I was to continue to pray for the bound and possessed and see them delivered. I was to continue to pray for the unsaved and see them find the Savior.

God continued, ". . .And thy power to every one that is to come."

I saw this as a command to teach young ministers of God's power. I was to become a teacher of young men and women: ministers, pastors, missionaries, and evangelists, about one thing—and that is God's power.

Now that I knew what my end-time ministry was to be, I must fulfill it. I must keep the faith. I must impart the faith.

In response to this direction from the Lord, I began the World Harvest Advanced School of Evangelism. Several times a year we would call ministers, missionaries, evangelists, and key laymen to South Bend for special studies regarding the greatest needs of the hour. Students came from across the United States as well as Africa, Europe, India, Latin America, Israel, Hong Kong, Okinawa, the Philippines, and many other countries to study God's Word.

By faith we built a lovely functional quarter of a million dollar facility with lecture hall, dining hall, dormitory rooms, and recreational area.

Soon it was evident that the Advanced School of Evangelism was not sufficient. We needed a regular Bible college. World Harvest Bible College has been in operation for a number years. It is a four-year resident training center providing preparation in the Word, plan, and work of God.

Experienced, Spirit-filled faculty are helping us develop a school that is measured by its distinctives. Through World Harvest Bible College the ministry is being multiplied many times over. We feel this will be one of the great outreaches to help us bring that million souls into the gates of heaven.

World Harvest Radio International

On December 25, 1985, LeSEA Ministries went live, 24 hours a day, via shortwave radio. WHRI radio enables us to reach more than 1.3 billion people daily with the gospel of Jesus Christ. We are heard in 117 countries such as Argentina, Israel, England, East and West Germany, Czechoslovakia, Denmark, Egypt, as well as the U.S.S.R. and many other countries that were long behind the iron curtain. Only God knows what a great harvest of souls this could bring not to mention uniting the body of Christ.

The End-Time Joseph Program to Feed the Hungry

I have only had three visions in my life, and I was well into my seventies before I had the last one.

I was sitting on the front row of a church in Panama City, Florida when, as I closed my eyes in meditation, I saw a River of Blood. It was as dramatic as the two other visions that I had seen.

I told the church and pastor about it that evening.

The following night in Birmingham, Alabama, as I was praying in church during the song service, I again saw in a strong manner this River of Blood. I thought it could mean judgment and so I told the people to pray and to write the date on the flyleaf of their Bibles.

The Tree of Life

A few days later I was in Denver, Colorado and a pastor said that the Lord had given him a prophecy concerning me.

He said my life was like a planted tree and that there were many branches on the tree.

He saw a limb representing the missionary churches I have raised up. He saw the branch representing the more than 100 different books and teaching syllabi I have written.

He saw the television stations as a limb on the tree.

He saw the Christian Center Church of South Bend as a strong branch.

Then he said, "Now a new branch will grow on your tree of life. It will be a large limb and more productive, with more satisfaction than any branch on your tree of life."

"The End-Time Joseph Program" the New "Branch"

I was leading a tour group in Jerusalem in November, 1987. One night I suddenly woke up at ten minutes to midnight, after going to bed at eleven p.m.

God said, "It is also midnight in prophetic time. One of My greatest concerns is that My people, part of My church, do not suffer death by starvation before I return. Will you help feed them?

"To them it would be an angelic food supply! It would be a miracle!

"Hunger is an agonizing death. Give to those who are dying and you shall live happily and victoriously.

"I speak to you in Jerusalem. It is the city where I took the bread and blessed it and said, 'Take eat, this is My body broken for you.' So take bread for the spirit, soul and body to the multitudes of the earth.

"Go especially to famine and war areas where there is devastation and hunger and feed them.

"Many are suffering. You will bring the food in fast by plane. You are to ride with the plane, watch the food being given out, and rejoice to see the children fed. Also give food to refugees who require help. It is My pity upon them.

"America has the food. Buy it and take it to the hungry.

"Use storage houses to hold the food until you are ready to distribute it to the hungry."

The Lord said, "If I bless you financially for your needs, will you operate a global feeding program for My people?

"You will distribute the food through pastors and churches. Don't let My people die of starvation."

My response at nearly five a.m., after listening to God for five hours, was: "I am willing Lord."

The Lord said, "Then you will understand, the River of Blood flowing toward you is life flowing deep and wide. At times the blessing will be almost uncontrollable. Get ready for it!"

The Three-Pronged Approach

To fulfill the vision God gave me, The End-Time Joseph Program to Feed the Hungry has a three-pronged approach that applies everywhere we go.

- Provide physical food.
- Pastors' seminars.
- Evangelistic crusades, praying for the sick and delivering the oppressed.

10,000 Pastors

God told me to call for 10,000 pastors to respond to the challenge of feeding the hungry. We have appointed pastors to act as international directors in various parts of the world. Using the three-pronged approach, wherever there is an emergency, our international directors deliver food and supplies to the local pastors who in turn distribute them to their own people.

King's Court and Queen's Court

In speaking to my heart, the Lord told me that this group of men would be called the "King's Court" and the women would be called the "Queen's Court."

We have developed parallel programs for men and women to be used in local churches. Men and women are challenged to pray and fast, to organize rallies and establish local fellowships to raise money for Feed the Hungry.

Fasting and Prayer

One of the ways we have found to be most effective in generating support for the millions who are starving, is to challenge people to fast two meals one day a week from sunset to sunrise and to give the money saved to feed the hungry. By denying ourselves food, we learn to have compassion for those who are starving.

Christian Center Church

Anything that is done for God should be centered in the church of Jesus Christ. Jesus said the gates of hell would not prevail against *His church.* Other para-church organizations are fulfilling a vital function, but none of these will ever replace the local church.

To be supported and backed by a strong church is necessary to all of our ministries. God has given us a great congregation that know how to pray and exercise faith in God. The Christian Center church family backing me in everything I do gives me a tremendous sense of strength and solidarity. One of the great blessings of my life is the privilege God has given me to be the shepherd of these beautiful people. It is a great joy to feel that the total outreaches of this ministry flow through a branch of the church of the Lord Jesus Christ.

As I write these words I feel strongly that all my life I have been in training. All that God has helped us accomplish has been in preparation for our greatest work immediately before us. Our faith is strong. The vision is clear. We are running fast. Our greatest hour is just ahead!

You can help Lester Sumrall
WIN A MILLION

God has called Lester Sumrall to win a million souls to Christ through the outreaches of the LeSEA ministry (Lester Sumrall Evangelistic Association). He showed him that the only way this would be possible is for friends and partners to work with him, pooling their resources to get the gospel out in every way possible.

When you join Brother Sumrall in this effort, you become a member of the Win-A-Million Club. Each month, your gift of $20 or more helps with these soulwinning outreaches:

Christian television channels:
KWHE-TV 14—Honolulu; KWHH-TV 14—Hilo
K21AG—Wailuku; *Ch. 35—Kailua Kona
KWHB-TV 47—Tulsa; *KWHR—Asia
KWHD-TV 53—Castle Rock/Denver
***Ch. 15—Grand Rapids; *Ch. 69—Oklahoma City**
WHKE-TV 55—Kenosha
WHME-TV 46—South Bend
WHMB-TV 40—Indianapolis
WHRI-East Shortwave; WHRI-South Shortwave
WHME-FM radio
Missionary Assistance
End-Time Joseph Program to
Feed the Hungry
World Harvest Magazine
World Bread (Feed the Hungry newsletter)
World Harvest Bible College—South Bend
Indiana Christian University, South Bend
24-Hour Prayerline (219) 291-1010
Christian Center School, South Bend
Audio and Video Teaching Tape Ministry
Books, tracts, pamphlets, teaching syllabi
Campmeetings—Conferences—Crusades

*under construction

As a Win-A-Million partner, you receive a beautiful gold lapel pin and the World Harvest Magazine. Simply write and say, "Here's my gift to help, I want to be a Win-A-Million partner."

Dr. Lester Sumrall
P.O. Box 12, South Bend, Indiana 46624

BOOKS BY DR. LESTER SUMRALL

- Adventuring With Christ
- My Story To His Glory
- Take It—It's Yours
- Gifts & Ministries Of The Holy Spirit
- Alien Entities
- Battle Of The Ages
- Beyond Anger And Pity
- Compulsive Desires
- Conscience—The Scales Of Eternal Justice
- Demons The Answer Book
- Bitten By Devils
- Ecstasy—Finding Joy In Living
- Faith To Change The World
- Faith Under Siege; The Life of Abraham
- Fishers Of Men
- Gates Of Hell
- Genesis—Crucible Of The Universe
- Hostility
- Hypnotism—Divine Or Demonic
- Imagination—Hidden Force Of Human Potential
- I Predict 2000 A.D.
- Jerusalem, Where Empires Die—
    Will America Die At Jerusalem?
- Jihad—The Holy War
- Living Free
- Making Life Count
- Miracles Don't Just Happen
- 101 Questions & Answers On Demon Power
- Paul—Man Of The Millennia
- Run With The Vision
- Secrets Of Answered Prayer
- Sixty Things God Said About Sex
- Supernatural Principalities & Powers
- 20 Years Of "I Predict"
- The Mystery Of Immortality
- The Making Of A Champion
- The Militant Church
- The Names Of God
- The Promises Of God
- The Dark Hole of World Hunger
    and the Christian Solution
- The Reality Of Angels
- The Stigma Of Calvary
- The Total Man
- The Will—The Potent Force Of The Universe
- The Human Body
- The Human Soul
- The Human Spirit
- Trajectory Of Faith—Joseph
- Three Habitations Of Devils
- Unprovoked Murder
- Victory And Dominion Over Fear
- You Can Conquer GRIEF Before It Conquers You
- You Can Destroy The Gates of Hell

LeSEA PUBLISHING COMPANY, INC.

P.O. Box 12, South Bend, IN 46624

1-800-621-8885